Order Of Battle

OPERATION OVERLORD

Utah Beach & the US Airborne Divisions

6 June 1944

James Arnold & Roberta Wiener

Ravelin

SHAEF

Supreme Headquarters Allied Expeditionary Forces

When Allied forces landed on the French coast on 6 June 1944, it marked the culmination of years of planning and preparation. Operation Overlord, the cross-channel assault against German-occupied France, was a more complex military endeavor than ever previously attempted. General Dwight D. Eisenhower arrived in London on 14 January 1944 to begin his new duties as Supreme Commander, Allied Expeditionary Force. He had just twenty weeks before the troops would load aboard their assault transports. He was the man charged with ensuring the invasion's success, and those weeks were full of important decisions. Initially there was a tremendous amount of inter-allied wrangling over plans and priorities, but soon Eisenhower forged a reasonably harmonious chain of command. British General Bernard L. Montgomery, in his role as head of the 21st Army Group, would take overall charge of the assault phase. On the American side, Lieutenant General Omar Bradley assumed operational control of the U.S. ground forces. Admiral Sir Bertram H. Ramsay served as Commander-in-Chief Allied Naval Expeditionary Force, while the senior American naval officer was Admiral Harold R. Stark. British Air Marshal Leigh-Mallory's Allied Expeditionary Air Force headquarters directed preliminary aerial operations against German targets in France and supervised the development of an overall air plan for the assault.

In final form, Overlord called for landing two field armies abreast in the Bay of the Seine west of the Orne river. While the British Second Army landed on three eastern beaches and took the key town of Caen, Bradley's First Army would assault two beaches west of the town of Port-en-Bessin. These beaches, code-named 'Utah' and 'Omaha', were chosen because they were within easy reach of tactical air support in England, were protected from westerly Channel swells by the Cotentin peninsula, and the six-fathom line ran near enough to shore to allow deep-draft attack transports to unload near the beach and to permit close in naval fire support. The VII Corps' objective was Utah Beach on the east Cotentin. Utah Beach would serve as an entry point for an attack against the port of Cherbourg. The build-up of allied forces in Normandy depended upon the early capture of this port.

By 4 June stormy weather had forced a postponement. Following this postponement, Eisenhower met with his invasion chiefs at 2130 on 4 June to set a new date. Weather reports indicated that conditions on 6 June would be barely tolerable. Cloud cover could impede allied bombers, interfere with airborne landings, and make naval gunfire spotting difficult. Choppy waves could disorder the landing craft. Admiral Ramsay reminded everyone that because of the strict naval time schedule they had only 30 minutes to make a final decision. Eisenhower refused to endorse a pessimistic view. In one of the most celebrated exchanges in military history, he turned to Montgomery to ask his advice. Monty replied, "I would say – Go!" At 2145, following some more discussion, Eisenhower announced his decision: "I'm quite positive we must give the order . . . I don't like it, but there it is . . . I don't see how we can possibly do anything else." This was Ike's finest wartime decision and because of it the largest fleet ever assembled, some 5,000 ships and craft, carried on toward their rendezvous with destiny on the Normandy coast.

The Supreme Commander's words would ring in the men's ears as their transports departed for the cross channel attack: "you are about to embark on the Great Crusade . . . Good Luck!"

Above: **General Dwight D. Eisenhower arrived in London on 14 January 1944 to begin his new duties as Supreme Commander, Allied Expeditionary Force. More than most high ranking American and British leaders, Eisenhower appreciated the potential of a vertical envelopment of the German position in France.**

Left: **The Allied command body for Operation Overlord was the SHAEF (Supreme Headquarters Allied Expeditionary Forces) under General Dwight D. Eisenhower (centre), the Supreme Allied Commander. Other SHAEF members were, from left to right, Lieutenant General Omar N. Bradley, Admiral Sir Bertram Ramsay, Air Chief Marshal Sir Arthur Tedder, General Sir Bernard Montgomery, Air Chief Marshal Sir Trafford Leigh-Mallory, and Lieutenant General Walter Bedell Smith.**

Planning for Overlord – Utah Beach and the US Airborne

VII Corps' target was Utah Beach on the east coast of the Cotentin peninsula. The corps' mission was to land on Utah to secure a foothold on the Normandy coast on the west side of the Vire river. The 4th Division with attached tanks and combat engineers would conduct the amphibious assault. Two pre-dawn airborne landings would support the beach landing. The 101st Airborne Division would descend southeast of Ste. Mère-Eglise to capture the vital exits from Utah Beach and to protect the eastern approaches to the beach. The 82d Airborne Division would land west of St. Sauveur-le-Vicomte with the mission of sealing the western approaches to the Cotentin peninsula.

Once safely ashore, VII Corps would advance on the key port of Cherbourg while its sister formation, V Corps, would advance deep into the bocage country. Then, joined by XIX Corps, the entire First Army would advance on a three corps frontage to the base of the Brittany peninsula. Joined by the Third U.S. Army, it would clear the peninsula, face east, and advance on Germany. Plans called for a lodgement over the Seine river by about D+90. General Omar Bradley and his lieutenants recognized that this ambitious plan was a broad maneuver scheme designed to help the logistical people plan, and was not an inflexible timetable.

The critical factors limiting how many First Army soldiers could attempt to land on D-Day were the number of amphibious assault vessels and the number of transport aircraft to carry the airborne forces. Both types of transport were in alarmingly short supply. The shortage of landing craft meant that planners had to devise strict priorities. Since they appreciated that they were conducting a frontal attack against a fortified position, they reduced the number of support troops and vehicles in order to increase the infantry's firepower. Rifle companies were organized into assault teams accompanied by equipment specially designed to help capture fortified positions. Each assault platoon would land with teams organized by function: rifle; wire-cutting; bazooka; flame-throwing; BAR; mortar; and demolition. Each platoon split into two assault sections composing one officer and 29 men, its size dictated by the 30-man capacity of the landing craft.

The final plan called for the naval task forces to transport, protect, and provide gunfire support for the landing forces. When the invasion convoy sailed, mine sweepers cleared and marked ten lanes through old German minefields in the Channel whilst fighter squadrons provided an air umbrella. Specially modified transports carried the assault force. They would arrive 11 miles off the Normandy coast and transfer the men into LCVPs and LCAs. These small craft, each carrying about 30 men, would form up in line abreast and head for the beaches. Meanwhile, the Navy would be completing its heavy shore bombardment.

Everyone realized that once the bow ramps opened, the infantry would have to conduct a frontal attack against a fortified position. Accordingly, each assault regiment had an attached tank battalion to spearhead the assault. The leading infantry wave would follow close behind the first tanks to clear the beaches. Under their cover the engineer demolition teams would cut and mark gaps through the beach obstructions before they became submerged by the rising tides. The engineers would be helped by special naval demolition units and tankdozers. Succeeding assault waves would carry mostly infantry and engineers with the latter tasked to clear remaining beach obstructions and then to accompany the infantry inland to perform any needed mine clearance. Planners calculated that the infantry would have secured the beach exits about three hours after H-Hour. At that time the heavy debarkation of vehicles would begin. After the assault sections cleared the beaches they would march inland to regroup into the standard battalion and regimental structure and then complete the tasks of securing and consolidating the corps' beachheads.

The 1939 U.S. Army Field Manual on strategy taught that "An objective may sometimes be gained through maneuver alone; ordinarily, it must be gained through battle." The Overlord planners understood that on the Normandy coast there was no chance to maneuver during the landing operation. It would take courage and brute strength to overcome the defenses.

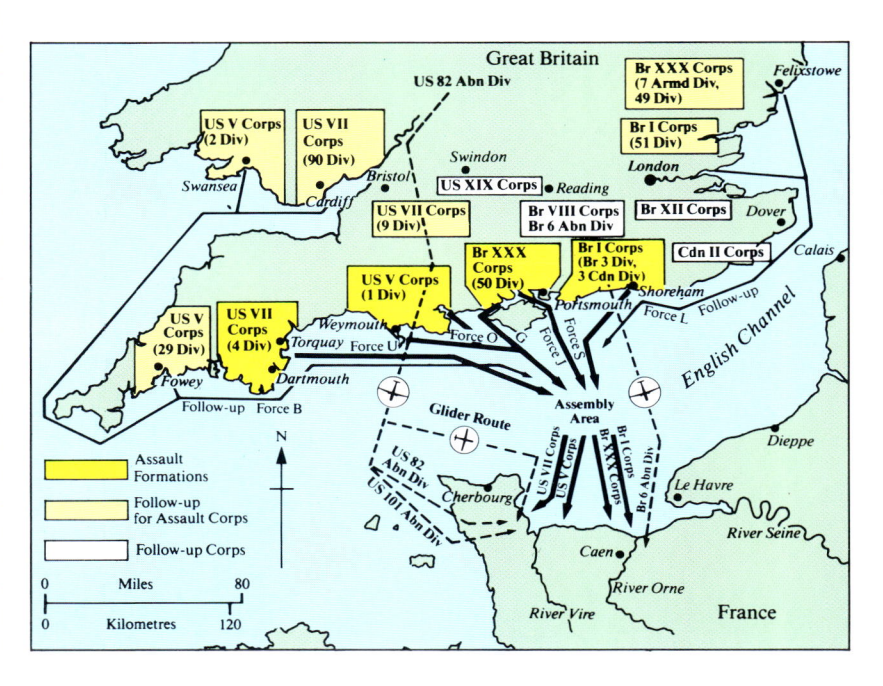

The invasion troops not stationed near England's south coast had to move to assembly areas. Here they received special equipment and waterproofed their vehicles. A second move brought the seaborne units of VII Corps to the Torbay area and east of Plymouth where they were near the embarkation ports. At the marshaling area they received final supplies, maps, and briefings. The units broke down into boatloads and waited for the word to move to the assault transports. The Utah invasion force assembled on 3 June. Because weather conditions forced a one-day postponement, the assault infantry had to remain cooped up aboard the transports for an extra day.

US First Army

Lieutenant General Omar N. Bradley assumed operational command of the American ground forces in the United Kingdom on 23 October 1943. Up to this date, the U.S. build-up had emphasized air forces and service troops. Henceforth until D-Day, an average of two American divisions per month arrived in the UK.

Bradley, like his 1915 West Point classmate Eisenhower, had missed overseas action in World War I. Between the wars he taught battalion tactics at the Infantry School, performed General Staff duties, and helped restructure the 82d Infantry Division into an airborne outfit. In 1943 he took charge of the IId Corps after Kasserine Pass. His complete overhaul restored that unit's battered pride. After Tunisia he led the corps into Sicily. Bradley's calm stability impressed everyone from General George Marshall down to the lowly private. This stability, combined with his combat experience, led him to the command of the 1st Army.

In 1938 the War Department General Staff said, "the Infantry Division continues to be the basic combat element by which battles are won, the necessary enemy field forces destroyed, and captured territory held." Bradley understood this and realized that the effort to secure a toehold in France might be very costly. He assumed that the divisions that arrived in the UK were fully trained. However, he recognized that the cross-channel assault involved unique technical challenges that necessitated special training. Thus, many assault units attended the renowned Assault Training Centre at Woolacombe. Here they practiced assaulting fortified positions and learned about amphibious assault doctrine. By the day of the invasion, Bradley knew that all of his forces were either battle-tested veterans or units fully trained for a cross-channel attack.

Bradley's army headquarters had to devise detailed assault plans, including regimental frontages and objectives, Ranger and airborne missions, fire support targets, the number of men to be landed on the first four tides, and the number

Debate about how best to utilize the airborne troops continued until 28 May, when a revised corps order established that both the 82d and 101st would land between Ste.-Mère-Église and Carentan. Here the 101st Division would secure the western ends of the causeways leading inland from Utah beach. These causeways traversed the flooded ground behind Utah Beach. The 82d would establish a defensive sector and a jumping off position for an advance on Cherbourg. The airborne landing with more than 13,000 men was the largest, most hazardous airborne operation in history to date.

Following the linkup with the airborne forces, the corps would clear the low, rolling country of the south Cotentin peninsula as far west as the Douve river. By D+2, optimistic planners envisioned a line running along the arc of St. Vaast-la Hougue – Valognes – St.-Sauveur-le-Vicomte. Then the 4th and 90th Divisions, joined by the 9th Division if necessary, would push the final 10 miles to Cherbourg. This port was badly needed to bring in the supplies required to nourish the army in Europe, and planners hoped the corps would capture it by D+15. Unforeseen by planners were the complications posed by the hedgerow country and earthen dikes used by Norman farmers to divide their fields and orchards.

of landing craft required, and submit these plans by February 15. It was a colossal chore. Once SHAEF set an invasion date, the army would begin a series of moves that brought its component parts closer to the embarkation ports. First they moved to concentration points where they received special equipment, waterproofed their vehicles, and lost personnel deemed unessential for the assault. Next, they moved to marshalling areas close to the port where they received final supplies, maps, tactical briefings, and divided into boatload-sized groupings. Task Force U, built around the 4th Infantry Division, would convoy the Utah Beach assault force. A total of 822 transport planes flying from nine airstrips in England would carry the airborne divisions.

Lieutenant General Omar N. Bradley was well liked by his men. Bradley took over operational command of the American ground forces in the United Kingdom on 23 October 1943. As of 1 January 1944, they numbered 749,298 men and eleven divsions and were, in order of arrival in the UK: 29th, 5th, 101st Airborne, 3d Armored, 28th, 2d, 1st, 2d Armored, 9th, 82d Airborne, and 8th Division. Of these, only four had seen previous combat. Although additional units would arrive before D-Day, including the lead infantry assault unit, the 4th Division, Bradley would have to conduct the cross-channel attack with a largely green force.

US FIRST ARMY
(Lieutenant General Omar N. Bradley)

US V CORPS [LANDED ON 'OMAHA' BEACH]
(Major General Leonard T. Gerow)

US 1st Infantry Division
(Major General Clarence R. Huebner)

US 29th Infantry Division
(Major General Charles H. Gerhardt)

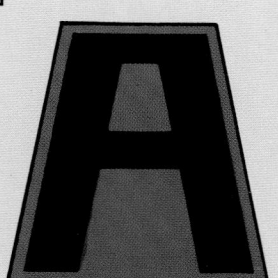

US VII CORPS
(Major General Joseph L. Collins)

US 4th Infantry Division
(Major General Raymond O. Barton)

US 82d Airborne Division
(Major General Matthew B. Ridgway)

US 101st Airborne Division
(Major General Maxwell D. Taylor)

US VII Corps

U.S. VII Corps arrived in the United Kingdom in October 1943 and immediately joined the First U.S. Army. In February 1944, Major General J. Lawton Collins took over command of the corps. Collins had commanded the famous 25th "Tropic Lightning" Infantry Division in the Pacific theater in 1942 and 1943. He had achieved a notable combat record during the Guadalcanal and New Georgia campaigns. His selection for corps command of VII Corps was due to his experience in amphibious assaults. For the cross-channel attack, the seaborne units of the corps composed Force U. Force U marshaled east of Plymouth in the Torbay region. At the end of April, Force U rehearsed the invasion during exercise Tiger conducted at Slapton Sands on the Devon coast. The exercise's conditions attempted to replicate as closely as possible the actual invasion. When two German E-boat flotillas attacked Force U and sank two fully loaded LSTs and damaged a third, the exercise became very real. More than 700 men, primarily engineers and quartermaster personnel, perished. Following this rehearsal, Force U had to endure nearly a month of anxious waiting. For security reasons they remained in marshaling areas behind barbed wire. Here they were guarded by 2,000 Counter Intelligence Corps soldiers who isolated them from all contact with civilians. To hide from German aerial reconnaissance the men practiced rigorous camouflage discipline. Force U began loading on 30 May at Plymouth, Dartmouth, Torbay, Torquay, Poole, Salcombe, Brixham, and Yarmouth. Its transports divided into 12 convoys. The USN *Bayfield* served as headquarters ship for Force U. The *Bayfield* dropped anchor in the transport area some 22,000 yards off Utah Beach, the best landing beach on the east coast of the Cotentin, at 0230, 6 June.

Confronting the corps on the beaches would be a network of German fortifications that were only about half complete. The German 709th Division had completed only one of forty-two planned positions. There was little defense in depth. In the Utah Beach sector, about 875 yards separated strongpoints and resistance nests.

Above: **Major General J. Lawton Collins took over command of VII Corps in February 1944. Collins had commanded the famous 25th "Tropic Lightning" Infantry Division in the Pacific theater in 1942 and 1943. His selection for VII Corps command was due to his experience in amphibious assaults. During the breakout from the Normandy beachhead and the pursuit across France, 'Lightning Joe' Collins would prove to be the army's foremost corps leader.**

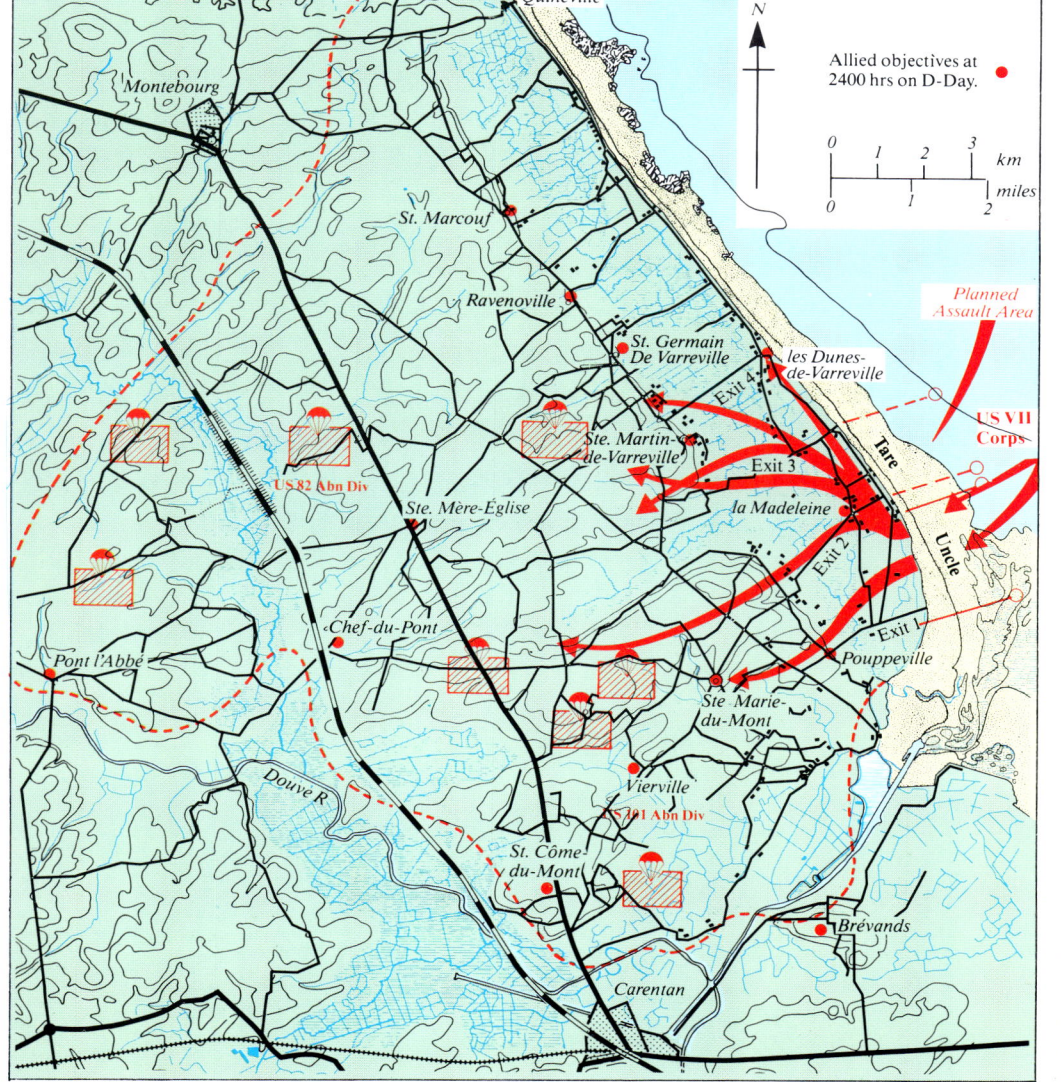

Left: **Because the Germans continued to modify their defensive dispositions, allied planning had to remain flexible. As late as 27 May, when General Collins learned that the German 91st Division had moved into the Cotentin, he had to revise the airborne plan. In final form, the Utah Beach plan called for dropping the 82d Airborne on both sides of the Merderet river while the 101st seized the western exits of the four roads leading from Utah Beach. The 4th Infantry Division, reinforced by attachments designed to assist the landing, would assault the beach.**

US First Army — Army Troops

In addition to the engineers working in the beach obstacle teams were those assigned to the 1st Engineer Special Brigade. This brigade included three engineer battalions belonging to the 531st Engineer Shore Regiment, a medical battalion, a joint assault signal company, a military police company, a DUKW battalion, an ordnance battalion, and various quartermaster troops. In order to reduce the risk of losing an entire unit if the transport craft sank, the engineers were to go ashore in a variety of landing craft. The plan called for the brigade to support the 4th Infantry's assault landing on Utah Beach. Each of two beaches, Uncle Red Beach on the left and Tare Green Beach on the right, were to be operated by a battalion beach group. As soon as the shore regiment's third battalion landed, a third beach, Sugar Red, would be opened.

Before the invasion the 1st Engineer Special Brigade possessed detailed intelligence regarding the progressive development of the defenses on Utah Beach along with detailed geographic and hydrographic studies. Maps showed German gun positions, minefields, beach obstacles, roadblocks, and anti-tank ditches. General Eisenhower worried greatly about the beach obstacle belt. In March, recon revealed that the Germans were planting obstacles on the tidal flats below the high water mark. To overcome all of this, the 1st Engineer Special Brigade, commanded by Brigadier General James E. Wharton, would assist the beach obstacle task force.

Wharton landed on Utah at 0730 along with the 1st and 2d Battalions, 531st Engineer Shore Regiment. They worked on widening gaps that the combat engineers had blown in the sea wall, clearing remaining mines, and improving the beach exits. Officers reconnoitered Sugar Red, a beach north of Tare Green, in preparation for the 3d Battalion's landing during the second tide. Meanwhile the 2d Battalion began to work on Sugar Red.

At 1400 Wharton established a command post near the entrance to Exit U-5 at La Grande Dune. He had expected twelve LCTs to deliver road building equipment. However, German shells hit three, and the tangle of offshore vessels prevented four others from beaching until D+1. Many engineer vehicles had been delivered into overly deep water and had their engines drowned when they tried to move to shore. Hauling these vehicles ashore under intermittent shell fire proved to be the heaviest engineering labor on D-Day.

By nightfall, the engineers had opened Sugar Red and made passable for vehicles the road leading inland from this beach. Wrecked vehicles and mines had been cleared and the existing lateral beach road had been reinforced with wood and wire matting. The military police assigned to the 1st Engineer Special Brigade helped direct traffic inland (1,700 vehicles landed during the fifteen hours following H-hour). Engineer, quartermaster, and ordnance men established dumps for ammunition and supplies. In sum, by day's end the brigade had established the basis for a supply organization that would nourish VII Corps during the entire Normandy Campaign. During D-Day the brigade lost 21 killed and 96 wounded, with most of the losses coming from German artillery fire.

The Sicilian and Italian beach assaults had been forced to contend with opposition from the Luftwaffe. To protect Utah Beach against similar trouble, elements of the 49th Anti-Aircraft Artillery Brigade were to land and establish gun positions on the beach. In the event, during the day only two German fighters attacked the American beaches. That night strafing German fighters did manage to conduct several attacks and inflict losses.

HQ, US First Army

Anti-Aircraft Artillery
49th Anti-Aircraft Artillery Brigade
  11th Anti-Aircraft Artillery Group
    Elements of the 116th Anti-Aircraft Artillery Gun Battalion
    474th & 535th Anti-Aircraft Artillery (Automatic Weapons) Battalions

Engineers
HQ & HQ Company of the 1st Engineer Special Brigade Group
531st Engineer Shore Regiment
HQ Detachment of the 191st Ordnance Battalion
  625th Ordnance Ammunition Company
HQ Detachment of the 577th Quartermaster Battalion
  3206th, 3207th & 4144th Quartermaster Service Companies
HQ Detachment of the 24th Transportation Corps Battalion
  462d, 478th & 479th Amphibious Truck Companies
HQ Detachment of the 306th Quartermaster Battalion
  556th and 557th Quartermaster Railhead Companies
  3939th Quartermaster Gas Company
4th Platoon of the 607th Quartermaster Graves Registration Company
HQ & HQ Detachment of the 490th Port Battalion
  226th, 227th, 228th and 229th Port Companies
HQ & HQ Detachment of the 518th Port Battalion
  298th & 299th Port Companies
1st Platoon of the 440th Engineer Depot Company

Signals
286th Signal Company
980th Signal Service Company

Chemical Troops
33d Chemical Company

Medical
261st Medical Battalion

Military Police
Company B of the 507th Military Police Battalion
449th Military Police Company

Miscellaneous
23d Bomb Disposal Squad
2d Naval Battalion

US VII Corps — Corps Troops

Traditionally the assault of a fortified post involves the art of the engineer. To allow VII Corps' infantry to conquer the West Wall, planners had allocated a large engineer component. First ashore would be the beach obstacle teams. Their task would be to cut and mark gaps through the belts of shore obstacles before a rising tide covered them. These teams comprised combat engineers and naval combat demolition units (NCDU). The assault gapping teams were composed of 27 men from an Army engineer combat battalion and a reinforced NCDU. Assigned one team to each gap, these teams would blow 50-yard-wide breaches in the beach obstacles. Assisting each gapping team would be a tankdozer to help clear the obstacles. In their wake would come eight support teams.

On D-Day, by 0715 the initial gaps were cleared. By 0930, Utah Beach was free of all obstacles. U.S. Army engineers in the beach obstacle teams lost six men killed and 39 wounded on D-Day. Their navy comrades lost four killed and 11 wounded. Because of their efforts, the entire 4th Infantry Division was able to land on D-Day.

Planners thought long and hard about the use of tanks during the assault. Finally, they decided to use the tanks not as an armored force but rather as close-support artillery. Tests showed that the Sherman tank's main gun could effectively neutralize or destroy concrete pillboxes by firing into their embrasures. Protected by this fire support, foot soldiers would cut their way through the wire entanglements to close in on and destroy the fortifications with flame throwers and demolition charges.

A tank battalion was attached to each assault regiment. These tanks would either swim ashore or land from LCTs. Unlike the British, American planners were only lukewarm about the prospects of the specially modified amphibious tanks. These were standard M-4 medium tanks (Shermans) fitted out with detachable canvas pleated screens to provide buoyancy. The screens could float the 32-ton tanks by displacement. The tanks had a duplex drive (thus their common name "DDs") consisting of twin propellers for swimming and the normal tank drive for land movement.

On D-Day, eight Landing Craft Tanks (LCTs), each carrying four DD tanks, were supposed to land the tanks at the same time the first infantry wave hit the beach. In the event, one LCT sank when it struck a mine and the remaining 28 tanks landed about 15 minutes after the first wave. At H+15, plans called for eight LCTs to land with tankdozers that the engineers would use to help clear obstacles. On D-Day, the tankdozers performed effectively by pushing some of the obstacles up onto the beach. However, the tried and true hand-placed charges accounted for most obstacles.

The tanks of the 70th and 746th Tank Battalions served with the spearhead of the 4th Division's inland drive. In a typical action, working inland from Exit 2, a lead tank of the 70th Battalion was knocked out by a mine. The second fell to an anti-tank gun. The third tank knocked out the gun and the infantry of the 8th Regiment continued on to its objective.

HQ, US VII Corps

Armor
HQ & HQ Company of the 6th Armored Group
746th Tank Battalion
70th Tank Battalion (Duplex Drive)
HQ & HQ Company of the 1st Tank Destroyer Group
801st & 899th Tank Destroyer Battalions

Artillery
HQ & HQ Battery of VII Corps Artillery
Detachment of the 13th Field Artillery Observation Battalion
29th, 42d, 44th and 980th Field Artillery Battalions
65th Armored Field Artillery Battalion

Engineers
HQ & HQ Company of the 1106th Engineer Group
49th Engineer Combat Battalion
238th Engineer Combat Battalion
HQ & HQ Company of the 1120th Engineer Group
Beach Obstacle Task Force
12 Naval Combat Demolition Units
237th Engineer Combat Battalion
One Company of the 299th Engineer Combat Battalion
582d Engineer Dump Truck Company
612th Engineer Light Equipment Company
991st Engineer Treadway Bridge Company
2062d Engineer FF Platoon
1605th Engineer Map Section
Company A of the 819th Aviation Engineer Battalion

Chemical Troops
87th Chemical Battalion

Signals
50th Signal Battalion
Detachment B of the 35th Signal Construction Battalion
Detachments of the 165th Signal Photo Company
Detachments B & C of the 175th Signal Repair Company
Detachment 2 of the 215th Signal Depot Company

Quartermaster
506th Quartermaster Car Company
3807th Quartermaster Truck Company
Detachments of the 385th and 3891st Quartermaster Truck Companies
1st Platoon of the 603d Quartermaster Graves Registration Company

Miscellaneous
47th Bomb Disposal Squad
six Surgical Teams of the 3d Auxiliary Surgical Group
187th Aviation Medical Disp.
Detachment of VIII Air Force Intransit Depot Group
Naval Shore Fire Control Parties
Air Support Parties

US 4th Infantry Division

Between the world wars, the 4th Division acquired its three infantry regiments, the 8th, 12th, and 22d, all of which dated back to the Civil War or earlier. The 4th Division was re-activated on 1 June 1940 at Fort Benning, Georgia under the command of Major General Walter E. Prosser, reorganized as the 4th Division (Motorized), and reorganized again as the 4th Motorized Division. It was redesignated the 4th Infantry Division on 4 August 1943 at Fort Dix, New Jersey. By that time it had had five different commanders, among them the famous Major General Terry de la Mesa Allen. Major General Raymond O. Barton, the 4th Infantry Division's commander on D-Day, had taken over the division in July 1942 and remained in command until December 1944. After participating in the IV Corps' Louisiana maneuvers, the 1st Army Carolina maneuvers, and the III Corps' Carrabelle maneuvers (in Florida), the 4th Infantry Division sailed to England in January 1944.

The division, with the 8th Infantry in the lead, met light resistance when it landed on Utah Beach for the 6 June 1944 invasion of Normandy. Brigadier General Theodore Roosevelt, Jr., assistant commander of the division, earned a posthumous Medal of Honor for his frontline leadership in the invasion of Normandy. Although he risked his life on Utah Beach, he died of a heart attack on 13 July.

Some of the hardest fighting during the invasion's first week occurred as the division fought toward the high ground along VII Corps' north flank around Quinéville-Montebourg-le Ham. The division assisted in taking Cherbourg on 25 June 1944, where it was relieved by the 101st Airborne. The division played a crucial role during the expansion of the bridgehead by spearheading the breakthrough into St. Lô by riding through enemy lines atop the tanks of the 2d Armored Division. The 4th then campaigned southward into France, taking part in the Cobra breakout of 25 July, and finally entered Paris with French Army units on 25 August 1944.

Continuing the offensive through France and Belgium, the first men of the division entered Germany on 11 September 1944, and broke through the West Wall on 14 September. The offensive slowed in the face of determined resistance.

In 19 days of heavy and costly combat, the 4th inched through Hürtgen forest, at one point advancing only 1.5 miles in 5 days. The Hürtgen forest proved a meat grinder for many American formations. The terrain greatly favored the defender. Here the 4th experienced some of the worst fighting of the war. The division was relieved by the 83d Infantry Division and withdrew to Luxembourg on 3 December.

The high command expected this to be a quiet sector, and that the division would be able to rest and refit after its ordeal. The tremendous German counteroffensive, the Battle of the Bulge, shocked everyone. The 4th Division held one shoulder of the "bulge". Its ability to prevent the German penetration from expanding toward Luxembourg City helped constrict the German operations to a narrow base. This in turn helped pave the way for General George Patton's 3d Army attack against the flank. As part of General Patton's thrust, the division captured Echternach on 27 December. The Battle of the Bulge was the U.S. Army's largest and most costly battle of World War II, and the 4th Division shared in the heavy losses of the Ardennes.

When relieved by the 87th Division on 17 January 1945, the 4th Division moved eastward, taking one town after another and on one day covering 20 miles. It crossed into Germany on 1 February, and penetrated the West Wall three days later.

The division crossed the Rhine on 30 March 1945 and the Main on 2 April. On 11 April, 4th division troops took both Rothenburg and Ansbach. It crossed the Danube river on 25 April and a few days later reached the Isar river bridges at Miesbach. There the division was relieved by the 101st Airborne on 2 May. The 4th then took up occupation duties under the 3d Army at Neumarkt on 4 May 1945.

The 4th Infantry Division sailed into New York Harbor on 10 July 1945 bearing gifts from the grateful people of Paris to the people of New York; a section of gate from the Tuileries and a stone cornice from the Hotel Crillon. The division returned to Camp Butner, North Carolina on 13 July, and was inactivated there on 12 March 1946.

In sum, the division participated in the Normandy, Northern France, Rhineland, Ardennes-Alsace and Central Europe campaigns of World War II. During the course of the war, the divi-sion lost 4,007 killed and 17,371 wounded, of whom 757 later died of wounds. The 8th Infantry Regiment received the Presidential Unit Citation for its conduct on the beaches of Normandy. Two men of the 8th Infantry and one of the 22d received Medals of Honor during World War II.

US 4th INFANTRY DIVISION
(Major General Raymond O. Barton)

8th Infantry Regiment
(Colonel James A. Van Fleet)

12th Infantry Regiment
(Colonel Russell P. Reeder)

22d Infantry Regiment
(Colonel Hervey A. Tribolet)

359th Regimental Combat Team [attached from the US 90th Infantry Division]
(Colonel Clarke K. Fales)

4th Cavalry Group
(Colonel Joseph M. Tully)

8th Infantry Regiment

Constituted in the Regular Army on 5 July 1838 as the 8th Infantry, the regiment was organized in New York state. It was assigned to the 8th Division in 1917, and to the 4th Division on 24 March 1923. The regiment's coat of arms recalls its New York origins, its service in the Mexican War, where it was the first American regiment to plant its colors at Churubusco, and its service in the Indian Wars, the Philippine insurrection, the war with Spain, and World War I.

8th Infantry Regiment

The 8th Infantry moved to Fort Benning, Georgia on 28 June 1940, participated in the Louisiana and Carolina maneuvers, transferred to installations in Georgia and South Carolina, and then sailed to England in January 1944. In England, the regiment, along with the other regiments of the division, attended the Assault Training Centre at Woolacombe, a beach on the south coast that replicated conditions in Normandy, and practiced amphibious assault landing techniques in preparation for its first combat of World War II.

The 8th Infantry Regiment, commanded by Colonel James A. VanFleet, led the 4th Infantry Division ashore at Utah Beach on 6 June 1944. It was the first unit among all the beach invasion forces to touch down on the coast of Normandy. After meeting only light enemy resistance on Utah Beach, the 8th Infantry went to the relief of the 82d Airborne at Ste.-Mère-Église. On the ensuing days it moved through the Cotentin peninsula, meeting heavier German resistance and taking many losses at Magneville and Écausseville. On 9 June the regiment engaged in costly fighting during the drive toward the Quinéville-Montebourg ridge. Notable was a Company L attack against the Magneville hangar featuring a charge across open fields under intense machine gun fire. The Regiment then held a defensive line at the le Ham-Montebourg highway until it joined its division's drive on Cherbourg on 19 June. On 21 June, the 8th, along with the 12th Infantry, attacked through the woods to the fortress walls of Cherbourg, penetrating the outer walls two days later. Cherbourg fell on 25 June, and the division remained there until relieved by the 101st Airborne.

The 4th Infantry Division spearheaded the breakthrough into St. Lô by riding through enemy lines atop the tanks of the 2d Armored Division. The 4th then campaigned southward into France, taking part in the Cobra breakout of 25 July, and finally entering Paris with French Army units on 25 August 1944.

Continuing the offensive through France and Belgium, the first men of the division entered Germany on 11 September 1944, and broke through the West Wall on 14 September. The 8th was stopped outside Brandscheid, and the division's offensive slowed in the face of determined resistance.

In 19 days of heavy and costly combat in November 1944, the 4th inched through Hürtgen forest, at one point advancing only 1.5 miles in 5 days. The 8th was cut off from the 22d on 19 November but was able to resume the attack three days later. The regiment reached the edge of the forest by 30 November but was stalled there. The Hürtgen forest proved a meat grinder for many American formations. Here the 4th experienced some of the worst fighting of the war. The division was relieved by the 83d Infantry Division and withdrew to Luxembourg on 3 December. On 7 December, the 8th Infantry was attached to the 83d Infantry Division until 12 December, when it rejoined its own division in Luxembourg.

Unfortunately for the 8th Infantry the German high command was about to launch Operation Herbstnebel in their very sector. The last desperate offensive, into the Ardennes, began on 16 December and the 8th was immediately in action. The 4th Division managed to hold the extreme right of the allied line, helping to prevent the German Seventh Army from developing their thrust south into Luxembourg. The position stabilized and Patton's 3rd Army now attacked the southern flank of the 'bulge', and the division captured Echternach and reestablished its position on the line of the River Sauer. The last major German counter-offensive had been repulsed, but it had cost the division dearly.

On 17 January 1945 the 4th Division was relieved by the 87th Division and went on the offensive, advancing at speed, crossing into Germany at the beginning of February and breaching the West Wall on the 3rd of that month.

The 8th assaulted the town of Prüm on 12 February. The division held the line at the Prüm river until making the crossing on 28 February. On 8 March, the regiment reached Honerath.

The division crossed the Rhine on 30 March 1945 and the Main on 2 April. On 17 April, the 8th Infantry took Ansbach. The division crossed the Danube river on 25 April, and two days later, the 8th established a bridgehead across the Lech at Schwabstadl. The division was relieved by the 101st Airborne on 2 May, and took up occupation duties under the 3d Army at Neumarkt on 4 May 1945.

The regiment returned with its division to New York on 10 July 1945, moved to Camp Butner, North Carolina a few days later, and was inactivated there on 25 February 1946.

The full 8th Infantry Regiment received the Presidential Unit Citation for its conduct on the beaches of Normandy. Two men of the regiment received the Medal of Honor during World War II for their conduct in the Hürtgen forest. In sum, the 8th Infantry Regiment participated in the World War II campaigns of Normandy, Northern France, Rhineland, Ardennes-Alsace, and Central Europe.

8th INFANTRY REGIMENT
(Colonel James A. Van Fleet)
  1st Battalion
  2d Battalion
  3d Battalion

12th Infantry Regiment

The 12th Infantry Regiment of World War II traces its lineage back to the 1st Battalion, 12th Infantry, constituted in the Regular Army on 3 May 1861 at Fort Hamilton, New York. It was redesignated the 12th Infantry in 1866, assigned to the 8th Division in 1917, and assigned to the 4th Division on 15 August 1927. In 1941 it was assigned to the 4th Motorized Division, which in turn was redesignated the 4th Infantry Division on 4 August 1943. The regiment's coat of arms recalls its first engagement at Gaines's Mill, Virginia in 1862 where it lost half its men, as well as its service in the Indian Wars, the war with Spain, and the Philippine insurrection.

After transfers to installations in Florida and South Carolina, the regiment sailed to England in January 1944. While in England, the regiment attended the Assault Training Centre at Woolacombe, a beach on the south coast that replicated conditions in Normandy, and practiced amphibious assault landing techniques in preparation for its first combat of World War II.

The 12th Infantry Regiment took part in the 4th Infantry Division's lightly contested 6 June 1944 assault landing on Utah Beach. Commanded by Colonel Russell P. Reeder, the 12th was to land at the center of the beachhead and secure a crossing over the Merderet. Marshy ground rather than enemy resistance delayed the regiment from its day's objective. In the ensuing days, the 12th attacked with its division toward the Quinéville-Montebourg ridge, and lost 300 men in a sharp battle near Emondeville. The regiment got so far ahead of its two sister regiments that it was ordered back on the defensive during 11-12 June.

In the division's attack on the defenses of Cherbourg, the 12th, abreast with the 8th, was ordered forward on 19 June but was unable to penetrate enemy defenses that night. On 21 June, the two regiments attacked through the woods to the fortress walls of Cherbourg. The 12th assaulted the defenses with tank support the next day, taking 800 prisoners on 23 June and another 400 on 25 June, the day Cherbourg fell. The 12th entered Cherbourg to clear the streets and sent one battalion to capture beach fortifications. The division remained there until relieved by the 101st Airborne.

The 4th Infantry Division spearheaded the breakthrough into St. Lô by riding through enemy lines atop the tanks of the 2d Armored Division. The 4th then campaigned southward into France, taking part in the Cobra breakout of 25 July, and finally entering Paris with French Army units on 25 August 1944.

Continuing the offensive through France and Belgium, the first men of the division entered Germany on 11 September 1944, and broke through the West Wall on 14 September. The 12th took heavy losses and gained little in the ensuing days, and the division's offensive slowed in the face of determined resistance.

In 19 days of heavy costly combat, the 4th inched through Hürtgen forest, at one point advancing only 1.5 miles in 5 days. The 12th was cut off by a strong German counterattack from 10 to 15 November. The Hürtgen forest campaign cost 33,000 casualties in two months. Along with other American units, the 4th Division experienced some of the worst fighting of the war. By 28 November, the 12th was finally able to link up with the 8th and 22d Regiments of the division. The 83d Infantry Division finally relieved the 4th Division, which was withdrawn on 3 December to north-east Luxembourg for rest and re-equipping.

The allied high command was aware that German forces were concentrating to the east in The Eifel. However under cover of bad weather, which neutralized the allies' command of the air, von Rundstedt launched 23 divisions (plus two in reserve) into the Ardennes.

On the far right of the allied lines the 212th Volksgrenadier Division attacked across the River Sauer, cutting off some elements of the 12th Infantry. Unsuccessful attempts were made to rescue the troops near Echternach. With the 8th and 22nd Infantry so far largely uncommitted, Major General Barton was able to concentrate a strong reserve and secure his defenses. To his left the 5th Infantry Division withdrew but then held firm preventing a German move south into Luxembourg. On the night of 18th General Bradley ordered Patton north. As part of his Third Army's offensive, the 4th Division took Echternach on 27 December.

On 17 January 1945 the 4th Division was relieved by the 87th Division and went on the offensive, storming into The Eifel and by the first week of February had crossed into Germany and burst through the West Wall.

The division crossed the Rhine on 30 March 1945 and the Main on 2 April. The 12th and 22d fought through the woods near Koenigshofen. On 17 April, the 12th took Rothenburg. The division crossed the Danube river on 25 April, and a few days later the 12th and 22d reached the Isar river bridges at Miesbach. There the division was relieved by the 101st Airborne on 2 May. The 4th then took up occupation duties under the 3d Army at Neumarkt on 4 May 1945.

The regiment returned to New York on 12 July 1945, moved to Camp Butner, North Carolina a few days later, and was inactivated there on 27 February 1946.

The full regiment received the Presidential Unit Citation for its conduct in Luxembourg. In sum, its World War II campaigns were: Normandy, Northern France, Rhineland, Ardennes-Alsace, and Central Europe.

12th INFANTRY REGIMENT
(Colonel Russell P. Reeder)
1st Battalion
2d Battalion
3d Battalion

22d Infantry Regiment

The 22d Infantry Regiment of World War II traces its lineage back to the 3 May 1861 Regular Army, where it was constituted as the 2d Battalion, 13th Infantry. Organized at Dennison, Ohio in 1865, the unit was redesignated the 22d Infantry in 1866. The 22d was assigned to the 4th Division in 1923. The regiment's coat of arms recalls its service in the Indian Wars, the war with Spain, and the Philippine insurrection.

After being briefly redesignated as a motorized regiment, the unit became the 22d Infantry Regiment on 1 August 1943. During 1941-1943, the 22d occupied duty stations in Alabama, Georgia, New Jersey, Florida, and South Carolina. The regiment sailed to England in January 1944. In England, the regiment attended the Assault Training Centre at Woolacombe, a beach on the south coast that replicated conditions in Normandy, and practiced amphibious assault landing techniques in preparation for its first combat of World War II.

The 22d Infantry, commanded by Colonel Hervey A. Tribolet, was the second regiment of the 4th Infantry Division to land in the 6 June 1944 assault on Utah Beach. The marshland more than enemy resistance impeded their movement on the first day of the invasion. In the ensuing days the regiment advanced on Crisbecq, and, during the drive on the Cotentin peninsula, captured Ozeville and Azeville fort. On 9 June, the 22d's attack against the Azeville blockhouse encountered a tenaciously defended fortified position. When demolition charges, bazooka, and tank fire failed, Private Ralph G. Riley delivered pointblank flamethrower fire that forced the defenders to surrender and thereby earned the Silver Star.

Abreast with its sister regiments, the 22d moved toward the Quineville-Montbourg ridge, making slow progress. On 20 June, the 22d advanced with its division for the first attacks on the Cherbourg defenses, with the assignment of cutting the Cherbourg road and occupying a hill near the airfield. The regiment met heavy but disorganized enemy resistance, and was briefly surrounded on 22 June. The division succeeded in taking Cherbourg on 25 June 1944, and the 22d spent two days mopping up the last enemy resistance around the airfield and the coastal batteries. The 101st Airborne relieved the 4th division at Cherbourg several days later, freeing them to continue advancing southward.

The division spearheaded the breakthrough into St. Lô by riding through enemy lines atop the tanks of the 2d Armored Division. The 4th then took part in the Cobra breakout of 25 July, and finally entered Paris with French Army units on 25 August 1944. On 11 September, a patrol from the 22d Infantry was among the first American troops to enter Germany. The division broke through the West Wall on 14 September, but it was stalled by enemy resistance, and the 22d was unable to capture Brandscheid.

The dense and fortified Hürtgen forest proved a bitter experience for many American formations and here in cycles of attack, retreat and counter-attack, the 4th Division experienced some of the worst fighting of the war. The Germans could not evict the invaders, but they could, and did, make the smallest gain very costly. By 29 November 1944, the 22d Infantry captured Grossahau in a hard-fought frontal assault. The division was relieved by the 83d Infantry Division and withdrew to Luxembourg on 3 December. The 22d was briefly attached to the 83d Division and did not rejoin its own division in Luxembourg until 12 December.

Little action was expected in this area, where the combat weary veterans of the 4th were to rest and refit after the bloody battles of November. Hitler's final daring gamble for victory in the West – the Ardennes Offensive – shocked everyone. The 4th Division were assaulted by units of the German Seventh Army, across the Sauer river. Through bitter fighting the 4th held the southern shoulder of the Ardennes 'bulge', blunting the offensive and forcing the Germans to operate on a narrow base. This helped facilitate General Patton's 3d Army attack against that flank, and, as part of this thrust, the division captured Echternach on 27 December.

The Battle of the Bulge was the most costly battle of World War II for the US Army with 8,497 killed, 46,000 wounded and 21,000 missing or POWs. The 4th Division shared these losses.

The 4th Division was relieved on 17 January 1945 and attacked eastward towards the Rhine. It entered Germany and infiltrated the West Wall by the beginning of February.

The division crossed the Rhine on 30 March 1945 and the Main on 2 April. The 22d, along with the 12th, fought through the woods near Koenigshofen. The division crossed the Danube river on 25 April, and a few days later the 22d and 12th reached the Isar river bridges at Miesbach. There the division was relieved by the 101st Airborne on 2 May. The 4th then took up occupation duties under the 3d Army at Neumarkt on 4 May 1945.

The 22d returned to New York on 12 July 1945 and moved to Camp Butner, North Carolina the next day. It was inactivated there in March 1946.

The regiment received Presidential Unit Citations for Hürtgen forest and St. Gillis-Marigny, and the 3d Battalion received the Presidential Unit Citation, streamer embroidered Carentan. One man of the regiment received the Medal of Honor for his conduct in the Hürtgen forest. In sum, the 22d Infantry Regiment participated in the World War II campaigns of Normandy, Northern France, Rhineland, Ardennes-Alsace, and Central Europe.

22d INFANTRY REGIMENT
(Colonel Hervey A. Tribolet)
1st Battalion
2d Battalion
3d Battalion

359th Regimental Combat Team

The 359th Infantry Regiment was constituted in the National Army on 5 August 1917, assigned to the 90th Division, and organized at Camp Travis, Texas a month later. The regiment's coat of arms commemorates its service in World War I. On 25 March 1942, the regiment resumed active service at Camp Barkeley, Texas. It departed for England in March 1944, arriving on 5 April.

Under command of Colonel Clarke K. Fales, the regiment was attached to the 4th Infantry Division for the 6 June 1944 landing on Utah Beach. The 359th came ashore amidst only intermittent shelling at Tare Green and, flanked by the 12th and 22d Infantry Regiments, advanced inland to the area of Foucarville.

Reunited with the 90th Infantry Division when it arrived in Normandy on 10 June, the 359th took part in the division's offensive actions in France. Fighting with the 9th Infantry Division, the 359th established a bridgehead across the Douve on 16 June.

As the 90th division assaulted the German positions west of Metz, the 359th tried and failed to take Fort Jeanne d'Arc on 15-17 September 1944 and was stalled in the 26-27 September battle of Gravelotte-St. Hubert Farm Road. The regiment assaulted across the Moselle with the 358th Infantry on 9 November 1944, pursued the Germans as far as the Nied River on 18 November, and advanced into Germany on 25 November. In December 1944, the 359th with its division shared the fight across the Saar, contesting the Dillingen bridgehead and West Wall fortifications, and withdrew on 19 December, regrouping back in France on 22 December 1944. The 359th fought in the Ardennes with its division from 9 January 1945, re-entering Germany on 31 January and taking Gros Langenfeld on 1 February.

During the renewed offensive across Germany, the 359th was attached to the 4th Armored Division 16-19 March 1945 and the 26th Infantry Division 5-10 April 1945. On 7 May 1945, it entered Czechoslovakia and was advancing toward Prague at war's end. The regiment returned to the United States from Germany on 24 December 1945 and was inactivated two days later.

U.S. decorations received by the 359th for service in World War II include: Presidential Unit Citation, streamer embroidered Pretot France (1st Battalion); Presidential Unit Citation, streamer embroidered Northern France (1st Battalion); Meritorious Unit Commendation, streamer embroidered European Theater 1944-1945.

359th REGIMENTAL COMBAT TEAM
[attached from the US 90th Infantry Division]
(Colonel Clarke K. Fales)

4th Cavalry Group

On 21 December 1943, the 4th Cavalry Regiment (Mechanized), stationed in England, was redesignated the 4th Cavalry Group. The 4th and 24th Cavalry Reconnaissance Squadrons were attached to the group at that time. In late 1943 and early 1944, all non-divisional mechanized cavalry regiments were broken into groups and squadrons. Their purpose was to use infiltration tactics, fire, and maneuver to conduct reconnaissance missions, joining combat only when necessary to complete a mission. Each cavalry group consisted of a Headquarters and Headquarters Troop, and at least two attached mechanized reconnaissance squadrons and was usually attached to a division for operations.

On 6 June 1944, two hours before H-Hour, detachments of the 4th and 24th Cavalry Squadrons led by Lieutenant Colonel E.C. Dunn came ashore to neutralize a suspected enemy presence on the St. Marcouf islands. Four men armed with knives swam ashore to mark the beaches and found the islands unoccupied. The remainder of the 132-man force completed the landing by H minus 1. Mines and artillery fire killed two and wounded 17.

The 4th Cavalry Group participated in the fight for Cherbourg, with its 24th Cavalry Squadron screening the 4th Division's right flank while the 4th Cavalry Squadron lined up to attack between the 9th and 79th Divisions. The group was then attached to the 2d Armored Division during the battle for St. Lô. Assigned to protect the flank of VII Corps, the group received a battalion of light tanks, motorized artillery, tank destroyers, extra infantry, and three engineer battalions. With this force it was to keep contact with Patton's rapidly advancing Third Army and to establish a bridgehead over the Meuse river at Mézières. The group entered Belgium on 3 September 1944 and Germany on 14 September.

The group moved into the Hürtgen forest in November, and then received the assignment of maintaining contact between the 2d Armored Division and the 8th Infantry Division during the Ardennes counteroffensive, re-entering Belgium on 22 December 1944. The 4th Cavalry Group advanced into Germany on 4 February 1945 and crossed the Roer river, crossed the Rhine at Bonn, and helped seal the Ruhr pocket by setting up roadblocks and clearing villages against bitter resistance. The unit remained in Germany and was redesignated the 4th Constabulary Regiment there on 1 May 1946.

4th CAVALRY GROUP
(Colonel Joseph M. Tully)
 4th Cavalry Squadron
 24th Cavalry Squadron

THE BATTLES — 8th Infantry Regiment

The 20 small craft, each holding a 30-man assault team and carrying the 8th Infantry's 1st and 2d Battalions, launched in sheltered waters and did not experience much difficulty with wind and surf. Still, the troops landed almost 2,000 yards south of the intended landing sector. This fortuitous error brought them in against a weakly defended beach. The 32 amphibious tanks intended to support the first infantry wave landed 15 minutes late because of the loss of their control vessel, and with the loss of four tanks. The lack of German opposition meant that the tanks were not immediately needed. The first wave, under the energetic direction of Brigadier General Theodore Roosevelt, Jr., the assistant divisional commander who this day would win the Medal of Honor for gallant leadership in the face of enemy fire, quickly reconnoitered and reorganized. There was some discussion whether to land the followup waves on the correct beach or whether to have them land on the existing beachhead. Roosevelt told the commander of the 1st Engineer Special Brigade, "I'm going ahead with the troops. You get word to the Navy to bring them in. We're going to start the war from here." After company-size task forces eliminated the lightly defended fortifications guarding two central beach exits, the 1st Battalion exited the beach in the direction of Audouville-la-Hubert while the 2d turned to the south to move along the Pouppeville road.

Five to fifteen minutes after the first assault wave landed, elements of an ad hoc Beach Obstacle Demolition Party hit the beach. So light was German opposition that, except for a shell that hit a landing craft just as it dropped its ramp and killed six Army engineers, all of the men assigned to demolition work got safely ashore. They abandoned the plan to clear lanes through the obstacles and instead began to clear the entire beach. This they accomplished within an hour. Companies A and C of the 237th Engineer Combat Battalion proceeded to blow gaps in the sea wall behind the beach and to remove mines.

Above: **US infantry transfer from their Coast Guard LCI (Landing Craft Infantry) to assault craft for the final run-in to the Normandy beaches.**

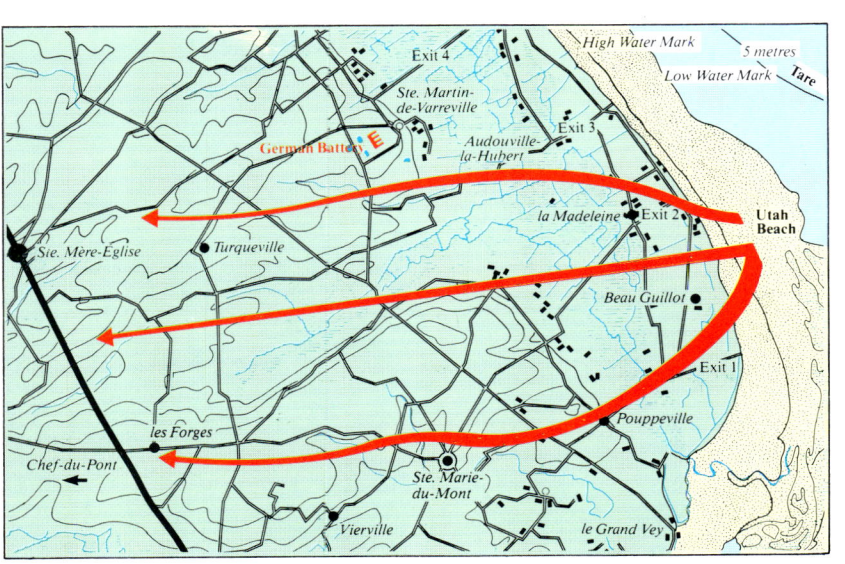

Of the 400 men assigned to the Beach Obstacle Task Force, 6 were killed and 39 wounded.

The second assault wave comprising the 8th Infantry's 3d Battalion and the 70th Tank Battalion landed in fine order on the beach. Well ahead of schedule, the beach area had been cleared and troops were moving toward their inland objectives. While moving along the causeway to Exit 2, the lead tank struck a mine. A German anti-tank gun claimed a second tank. A third tank advanced to knock out the anti-tank gun and the column pushed until just north of Ste. Marie-du-Mont where it encountered a dug-in German force backed by 88mm guns. A short fire-fight ensued and the 3d Battalion closed in, cutting down some 50 Germans who broke and ran. By nightfall the battalion was north of les Forges facing the high ground south of Ste.-Mère-Église. Meanwhile the 1st Battalion had moved west on the causeway to Exit 3, crossed the flooded ground, and approached Turqueville by evening.

The 2d Battalion's Company F dealt with the beach defenses. Company E found a trail through the mine field behind the dunes and followed it inland. Battalion commander Colonel MacNeely then maneuvered Company E behind Company F and led it along the road on the eastern edge of the flooded area. Company G moved south behind the shelter of the sea wall. This sidle south toward the battalion's D-Day objectives took place under continuous small arms fire. Enemy shell fire brought Company G to a brief halt as it neared a strong point at Beau Guillot. It pressed on and joined the balance of the battalion at Pouppeville. Here, shortly before noon, the 2d Battalion met elements of the 501st Parachute Infantry. It marked the first link up between the seaborne and airborne troops. The battalion continued west and bivouacked near the road intersection at les Forges for the night.

The 8th's inland advance had bypassed enemy positions around the lock north of le Grand Vey. This was an important position because it controlled the inundations. Company A, 49th Engineer combat Battalion undertook the mission of securing this lock and reducing the adjacent defenses. The company captured the position and took 28 prisoners. The next day it would seize the strongpoint at le Grand Vey and capture another 59 prisoners, 17 tons of ammunition, and three artillery pieces.

With the help of the engineers, the 8th Infantry had reached all of its D-Day objectives. The 2d and 3d Battalions supported by elements of the 70th Tank Battalion had a solid defensive position at les Forges with patrols pushed out aggressively toward Chef-du-Pont. The 1st Battalion along with the 70th's Company A was facing the German strongpoint at Turqueville. The relative ease of the landing surprised the regiment. Along with the 22d Infantry, the 8th suffered only 197 casualties including 12 men killed.

THE BATTLES: 12th Infantry Regiment

A mile or so behind the dunes backing Utah beach was a water barrier extending from Quinéville on the north to Pouppeville on the south that the Germans had created by reversing the action of a system of locks that the French had built to drain the land. Seven causeways crossed the flooded ground, connecting the beach with a north-south inland road.

Colonel Russell P. Reeder's 12th Infantry was supposed to land after H+4 hours and advance inland to capture the high ground between Émondeville and the Merderet river and to seize a crossing over the Merderet at le Port Brehay. When they began to land, shortly after noon, they encountered a situation somewhat unlike that for which they had trained. All the beach obstacles had been cleared. There was little German resistance beyond an occasional random shell burst. So the regiment rallied on the beach and set off across the inundated ground toward their objective. The major obstacle proved to be the waist-deep water and the numerous ditches and holes that swallowed the heavily burdened soldiers. After crossing the flooded region, the 12th Infantry joined the 502d Parachute Infantry south of Beuzeville-au-Plain. Here it took up overnight positions confronting the German strongpoint in the village. While the paratroopers secured the regiment's left flank, its left rear remained a trouble spot since Germans continued to defend a strongpoint around Turqueville. The right flank was trouble free with 22d Infantry's 1st and 2d Battalions in comfortable defensive positions facing Foucarville. The 12th Infantry Regiment as a whole suffered fewer than 80 casualties on D-Day.

The Germans had prepared for more than two years to repel an allied landing in France. Yet on 6 June 1944, the 4th Division managed to carve out an extensive bridgehead with relative ease. The division's efforts routed the myth of the impregnability of Rommel's Atlantic Wall. Not only had the 4th Division landed with small loss, but VII Corps as a whole had managed to build a considerable bridgehead in short order. Excepting the 20th Field Artillery Battalion, the entire division had landed in the first fifteen hours. In addition, safely ashore were one battalion of the 359th Infantry, the 65th Armored Field Artillery Battalion, 87th Chemical Mortar Battalion, 899th Tank Destroyer Battalion (minus two companies), the 70th and 746th Tank Battalions, and components of the 1st Engineer Special Brigade. Already this engineer force had begun organizing the beach to support the buildup. More than 20,000 VII Corps soldiers and 1,700 vehicles landed on Utah Beach by the end of the first day.

Why had this success occurred? First, because of systematic British and American elimination of the German weather forecasting stations, the Germans had not shared the allied ability to predict weather conditions on the Normandy coast. They believed 6 June unsuited to an invasion.

Above: **Men of the 4th Infantry Division take cover on Utah Beach during D-Day.**

Thus, the 12th Infantry and its sister formations had achieved tactical surprise.

Second, German preparations were far from complete when the 4th Division stormed ashore. Total allied dominance in the air prevented the Germans from using the railroads to carry adequate *matériel* to the Normandy coast to build fortifications. A brilliant allied deception plan left German strategists believing that the major cross-channel attack would be led by George Patton and would land at the Pas de Calais. For weeks after the landing, Hitler and his generals continued to believe that the Normandy landing was a diversion in favor of the main effort to be delivered elsewhere.

Lastly, there was a huge dispute among German strategists regarding the proper way to defeat the invasion. One faction believed that the best solution was to concentrate German panzer forces well inland. Once the axis of the allied attack was clear, this panzer force would move to the coast and deliver a crushing counterattack. Rommel, with his experience in the North African desert, understood that total allied mastery of the air demanded unorthodox German methods. Thus, this master of the armored assault believed that the best way to use the panzers was to place them just behind the beaches from where they could deliver an early counterattack. Rommel put his faith in a system of fixed fortifications designed to stop the invasion in its tracks at the water's edge.

His vision may have been militarily sage, but it ignored reality. Forced to fight the Russians along the vast Eastern front, unable to sustain the effort he required to build an Atlantic Wall according to specifications, Rommel's solution failed in the face of the 4th Division's assault. The ease with which the 12th Infantry advanced off Utah Beach demonstrated the fallacy of the Rommel approach.

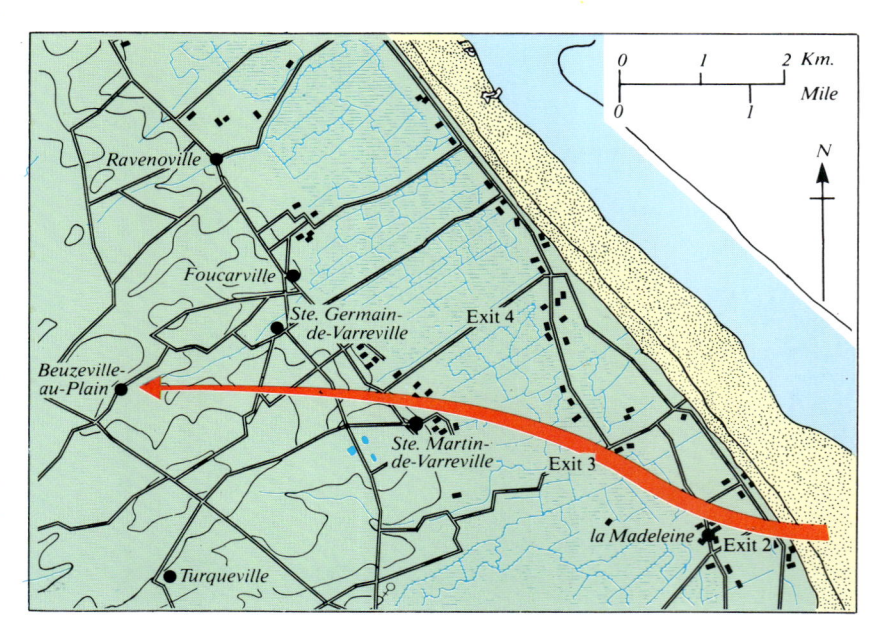

THE BATTLES 22d Infantry Regiment

Just after Pearl Harbor, Brigadier General Dwight D. Eisenhower had told his staff "We've got to go to Europe and fight." On 6 June 1944, the soldiers of the 22d Infantry Regiment, commanded by Colonel Hervey A. Tribolet, were ready to implement Eisenhower's vision. They began to land at Utah Beach at H + 85 minutes. The plan called for the regiment to turn north from the beach and seize the causeway across the flooded fields at les Dunes de Varreville. Then the regiment was to push northwest to capture the high ground around Quineville and Fontenay-sur-Mer. The unit landed cleanly on Utah Beach because of some superb engineer work that had paved the way.

The combat engineers of the Beach Obstacle Task Force along with the Naval demolition teams had accomplished more than anticipated. The naval troops were responsible for destroying all obstacles under water while the army troops took care of the rest. Their initial responsibility was to blow four 50-yard wide gaps in the German obstacle belt. Aerial photos had indicated that there was a triple band of obstacles at water's edge. Wading ashore with some 60 pounds of explosives each, the engineers found that the number of obstacles was fewer than expected. Instead of limiting themselves to the designated task, they opted to widen the lanes through the obstacles to accommodate the press of landing craft that was gathering offshore. Relying primarily on hand-placed demolition charges connected with primacord, they had blown huge lanes in the obstacle belt in spite of moderate German artillery fire. By 0930 Utah Beach was free of all obstacles. Thereafter, the engineers concentrated on blowing gaps in the sea wall, creating lanes through the sand dunes, and clearing the exit roads across the flooded land just inland from Utah Beach.

Consequently, when the 3d Battalion, 22d Infantry landed on Green Beach about 0745 as part of the second wave, it found itself able to proceed as planned. It moved north along the beach to eliminate any enemy strongpoints that could deliver effective fire against the beach. Around 1000 troops, the regiment's 1st and 2d Battalions touched shore. The plan called for them to march inland through Exit 4. However, this exit's eastern end was still covered by German fire while the exits to the south were full of other divisional troops. As a result, the two battalions did not use the causeways and began to wade through the flooded zone between the exits. When the regiment had to cross the Exit 3 road in order to advance toward its objective, St. Germain-de-Varreville, it encountered elements of the 8th Infantry using the road. The resultant congestion delayed everyone.

The traffic problem stemmed from the fact that the initial landing had taken place some 2,000 yards away from the planned landing beach. The 1st and 2d Battalions spent about seven hours wading through the flooded zone before reaching dry land near St. Martin-de-Varreville. They moved on to St. Germain-de-Varreville where they settled in for the night.

Before them lay the village of Foucarville and on the left was the 12th Infantry which confronted a German strongpoint at Beuzeville-au-Plain. The 3d Battalion cooperated with 3d Battalion, 8th Infantry and the 70th Tank Battalion to complete the reduction of the German beach defenses. Thereafter it moved north past les Dunes de Varreville and the Exit 4 road. It reached the southern end of Hamel de Cruttes, another German strongpoint, by nightfall.

The regiment fell short of its D-Day objectives. However, the rapid inland push of the 22d Infantry was part of a broad allied advance on D-Day that put paid to German plans to repel the invasion at the water's edge. By D + 2, VII Corps would be in position a mere 10 miles from the key port of Cherbourg and ready to advance. Overall, once ashore, the allies could ultimately win the race to mass men and munitions in Normandy. The German high command calculated that the rate of allied buildup across Normandy's open beaches would be far slower than the rate at which German reserves could reach the front. Instead, the Germans had to transport units along roads and rail lines subjected to terrible aerial bombardment while the allies could bring divisions unchallenged from England to France.

Shortly after the landing, divisional commander Major General Barton visited one of his frontline battalions to spur it on. He assured them that they confronted only second-rate German units. A young lieutenant replied, "General, I think you'd better put the Germans on the distribution list. They don't seem to realize that."

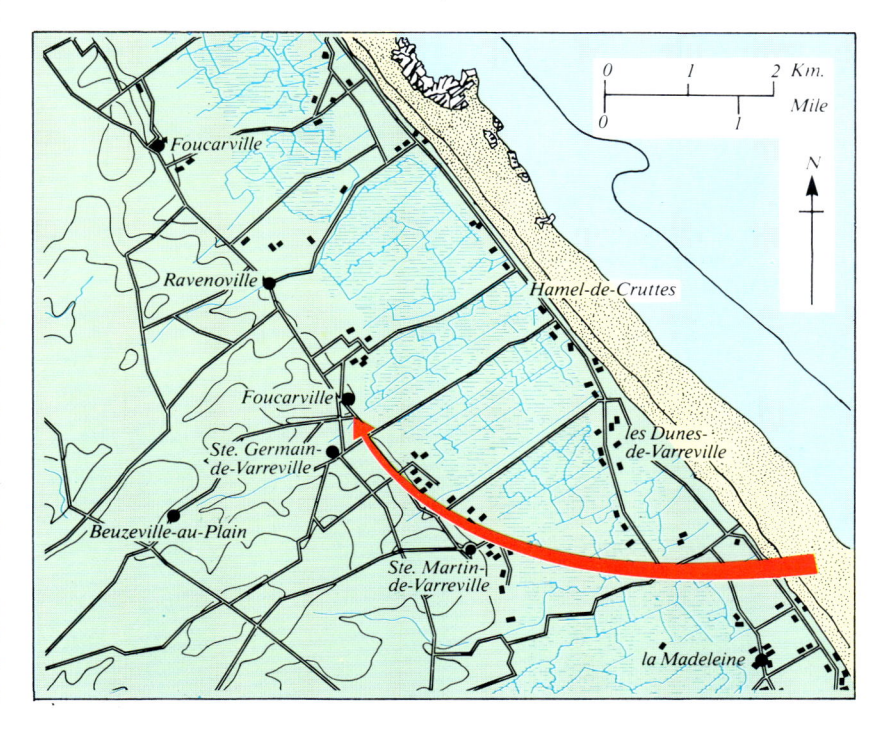

Above: **Medics give first aid to a wounded soldier on the beach near la Madeleine.**

US 82d Airborne Division

The 82d Infantry Regiment of World War I was the unit of the famed Sergeant Alvin York, who had singlehandedly captured 132 Germans. The "All-American" 82d Division was reactivated 25 March 1942 at Camp Claiborne, Louisiana under the command of Major General Omar N. Bradley and redesignated the 82d Infantry Division in May 1942. Converted to the 82d Airborne Division on 15 August 1942, it moved to Fort Bragg, North Carolina on 3 October 1942, and was placed under command of Major General Matthew B. Ridgway in June 1942.

The division sailed to Casablanca, landing in May 1943, and after a period of training, took part in the air assault of Sicily. The Sicilian operation was the first in which an entire airborne division took part. At the start of the campaign, several American planes that flew off course fell to friendly anti-aircraft fire. This loss influenced future airborne operations, causing planners of the Normandy invasion to route their flights well away from allied ships. On 9 July 1943, the 505th Parachute Infantry jumped over Sicily at midnight. Wind conditions scattered the parachutists over a 60-mile area. In some cases, disoriented pilots dropped their men at low altitude, causing a high incidence of jump injuries. As the paratroopers reassembled into small groups, they mingled with British troops, helping to capture Comiso, Noto, and Ragusa, and eventually made contact with the 1st Infantry Division. By 23 July, the division held the crossings of Fiume delle Canno and the Marsala-Trapani region on Sicily's western coast.

Prior to the invasion of Italy, General Maxwell Taylor, then the 82d Airborne's Chief of Artillery, was smuggled into Rome to confer with Italian officers. This meeting led Eisenhower to abort the air assault of Rome. The 82d invaded Italy on 13 September 1943 in both airborne and amphibious assaults near the Sele river, and occupied Naples by 1 October. When the bulk of the division returned to North Africa, the 504th Parachute Infantry stayed on to fight at Anzio. The division moved to the United Kingdom in December 1943 to train for the Normandy invasion. Because the 1st Army staff considered it a thoroughly battle-tested unit, the division did not attend the renowned Assault Training Centre at Woolacombe. In order to avoid the dispersion of force that had characterized previous airborne operations, the division received two additional parachute regiments for the assault.

In the early hours of 6 June 1944, the division's 505th Parachute Infantry Regiment, along with the attached 507th and 508th Parachute Infantry Regiments parachuted behind enemy lines near Utah Beach. Elements of the 325th Glider Infantry regiment arrived by sea and reinforced the paratroopers next day. The division returned to England for rehabilitation on 13 July 1944. Major General James M. Gavin, who as a colonel had led the 505th Parachute Infantry on their first combat jump into Sicily, assumed divisional command in August 1944.

Parachutists and glidermen of the division invaded Nijmegen-Arnhem by air on 17 September 1944. The 82d Airborne spent nearly two months in Holland, capturing the Maas bridge at Grave, the Maas-Waal Canal bridge at Heumen, and the Nijmegen-Groesbeek ridge, and attacking across the Waal river in assault boats.

The division was billeted in France for the winter until called upon to respond to the Ardennes counteroffensive on 17 December 1944. The 82d moved by truck to an area near Liège. The division attacked in the Vielsalm and St. Vith areas, forcing the enemy back. It lost Manhay and was in turned forced back from the Vielsalm salient on 25 December. The division fought its way past Bra, Salm, and Comte, finally capturing Heersbach on 28 January 1945. An action typical of the 82d paratrooper occurred in Belgium: as vehicles full of allied troops streamed out of a town under enemy attack, a paratrooper set up his bazooka by the roadside, declaring "The retreat stops right here."

On 2 February, the division joined the attack on the West Wall and then advanced on the Roer river, crossing on 17 February. After a period of rehabilitation in France, the 82d moved to the vicinity of Cologne and took up occupation duties on 4 April. They advanced to attack across the Elbe on 30 April.

The division set up its final wartime command post in Ludwigslust, where it accepted the surrender of the German 21st Army and liberated the Wobelein concentration camp. The 82d Airborne returned briefly to France to receive replacements and train, then went on to join the occupation force of Berlin in July 1945. The division returned to New York in January 1946 to a triumphal march up Fifth Avenue.

Over the course of the war, the division lost 1,619 killed and 6,560 wounded, of whom 332 later died of their wounds. Two men of the division won the Medal of Honor: one of the 508th Parachute Infantry and one of the 325th Glider Infantry, for his conduct in Normandy.

Major General Matthew B. Ridgway was a 1917 West Point graduate. He served in the War Department's War Plans Division from 1939 to 1942. Ridgway then became assistant division commander of the 82d Division when that unit was activated in March 1942. Three months later he was head of the unit. After the division converted to airborne, Ridgway led it in the Sicilian and Italian campaigns. When, on D-Day, his division experienced a scattered drop on the edge of the assembly area for the German 91st Division, Ridgway retained his composure. By relying on the small unit initiative characteristic of the airborne forces, his division clung to its position at Ste.-Mère-Église and along the Merderet river.

US 82d AIRBORNE DIVISION
(Major General Matthew B. Ridgway)

505th Parachute Infantry Regiment
(Colonel William E. Ekman)

507th Parachute Infantry Regiment
(Colonel George V. Millett, Jr.)

508th Parachute Infantry Regiment
(Colonel Roy E. Lindquist)

325th Glider Infantry Regiment
(Colonel Harry L. Lewis)

US 82d and 101st Airborne Divisions — Divisional Troops

The United States Army was a little slow to appreciate the potential of airborne forces. The manner in which the German army utilized such forces in its blitzkrieg against France in 1940 awakened many. The first Parachute Test Platoon was activated at Fort Benning, Georgia in June 1940. Still, it was not until 21 March 1942 that the Airborne Command became an independent entity. On that date it was activated from the Provisional Parachute Group. Before then, the airborne organization and training had been subsumed by the regular infantry establishment. The next month the command transferred from Fort Benning to Fort Bragg, North Carolina. The command had the responsibility to activate and prepare airborne units. To this end it formed the Parachute School on 15 May 1942. A February 1944 reorganization at Fort Bragg saw the Airborne Command become the Airborne Center. American planners initially believed that airborne forcesforces could be created as ad-hoc formations for particular missions simply by utilizing air transport for regular infantry and adding some parachute units. As planning for the invasion of France progressed, they realized that there was need for a more permanent organization. By mid-October 1942 planners had devised a formal table of organization for the airborne divisions.

As of June 1944, each airborne division had an authorized strength of 8,596 men. The parachute infantry regiments contained 1,884 enlisted men, 5 warrant officers, and 140 officers. Compared to standard infantry formations they were lightly armed. Providing the regiment experienced a perfect drop and recovered all equipment bundles, it carried into battle 132 light .30-caliber machine guns (they had none of the heavier .50-caliber models), 12 81mm and 27 60mm mortars. Some 495 men carried the .30-caliber carbine while the balance of the men were armed with the standard .30-caliber rifle. The glider infantry regiments had 1,602 enlisted men, 3 warrant officers, and 73 officers. Because they would land in gliders, they went into battle (again assuming a perfect, crash-free landing) more heavily armed than their parachute brethren. Each regiment landed with 3 heavy .50-caliber machine guns, 8 heavy .30-caliber machine guns, 12 light .30-caliber machine guns, 12 60mm mortars, 24 81mm mortars, and 81 2.36in anti-tank rocket launchers (bazookas). Because of these greater numbers of crew-served weapons, about four in ten glidermen (635 soliders) carried the .30-caliber carbine while the remaining 834 carried the standard .30-caliber rifle. A total of 530 men comprised a parachute infantry battalion while the authorized strength of a glider infantry battalion was 622.

The formal organization of the airborne division provided for glider field artillery battalions and parachute field artillery battalions. Both were equipped with light (for ease of transportation) 75mm pack howitzers. The pack 75mm howitzer and its ammunition could be broken down into nine loads that a 24-foot cargo-chute could carry. The division as a whole had 36 pack howitzers. Other airborne divisional troops included a signal

Attachments landed by air

HQs US 82d and 101st Airborne Divisions (–)

Artillery
377th Parachute Field Artillery Battalion
456th Parachute Field Artillery Battalion (–)
319th & 320th Glider Field Artillery Battalions

Anti-Aircraft Artillery
80th & 88th Anti-Aircraft Battalions
Batteries A & B of the 81st Anti-Aircraft Battalion

Engineers
Company C of the 326th Airborne Engineer Battalion

Medical
326th Airborne Medical Company (–)

Military Police
platoon of Military Police

Quartermaster
426th Airborne Quartermaster Company

Signals
Divisional Signal Companies (–)

Attachments landed on Utah Beach

HQs US 82d and 101st Airborne Divisions (–)

Infantry
325th Glider Infantry Regiment (–)

Artillery
321st & 907th Glider Field Artillery Battalions (–) (landed D+1 & D+2)
456th Parachute Field Artillery Battalion (–) (landed D+1 & D+2)

Anti-Aircraft Artillery
Batteries C, D, E & F of the 81st Anti-Aircraft Battalion

Engineers
Companies A & B of the 326th Airborne Engineer Battalion

Medical
326th Airborne Medical Company (–)

Military Police
platoon of Military Police

505th Parachute Infantry Regiment

The 505th Parachute Infantry was constituted in the Army of the United States on 24 June 1942 and activated at Fort Benning, Georgia on 6th July 1942 as part of the Airborne Command. It was assigned to the 82d Airborne Division and moved to Fort Bragg, North Carolina on 10 February 1943.

The 505th sailed to North Africa with the 82d Airborne, arriving at Casablanca in May 1943 for a period of training. The regiment parachuted into Sicily near Gela on 9 July 1943 and linked up with the 1st Infantry Division the next day. On 16 September 1943, the 505th parachuted into Italy near the Sele river by night to reinforce other units of the division.

After a training period in the British Isles, the three battalions of the 505th, commanded by Colonel William E. Ekman, parachuted behind enemy lines near Utah Beach on 6 June 1944. They landed northwest of Ste.-Mère-Église with the objectives of capturing the town, occupying Neuville-au-Plain, and seizing the La Fière bridge over the Merderet. On 7 June, the 505th seized Montebourg station, and on 16 June reached St.-Sauveur-le-Vicomte.

The regiment returned to England on 13 July 1944, took part in the air assault of Nijmegen-Arnhem on 17 September, and fought there until relieved on 11 November. The division was called to action in the Ardennes on 18 December. The division pushed the enemy back from the Vielsalm-St. Vith area two days later, and the 505th Infantry took the brunt of a German attack near Trois Ponts on 22 December 1944.

The regiment entered Germany with its division on 30 January 1945, returned to France 19 February, again moved to Germany on 2 April, where it continued to advance until war's end. The 505th returned to the United States with its division in January 1946.

The entire regiment received the Presidential Unit Citation and the French Croix de Guerre with Palm for its conduct at Ste.-Mère-Église in Normandy. The 2d Battalion of the 505th also received the Presidential Unit Citation, streamer embroidered Nijmegen. In sum, the World War II campaigns of the 505th were: Sicily, Naples-Foggia, Normandy, Rhineland, Ardennes-Alsace, and Central Europe. The regiment's coat of arms recalls its first combat in Sicily in World War II.

505th PARACHUTE INFANTRY REGIMENT
(Colonel William E. Ekman)
  1st Battalion *(Lt Col Frederick C.A. Kellam/Lt Col Mark S. Alexander)*
  2d Battalion *(Lt Col Benjamin H. Vandervoort)*
  3d Battalion *(Lt Col Edward C. Krause/Maj William J. Hagan)*

507th Parachute Infantry Regiment

The 507th Parachute Infantry was constituted in the Army of the United States on 24 June 1942 and activated at Fort Benning, Georgia as part of the Airborne Command. It was assigned to the 1st Airborne Infantry Brigade on 14 April 1943 at Alliance Army Airfield, Nebraska. In December 1943, the regiment arrived in England. It was attached to the 82d Airborne from 14 January until 27 August 1944.

The regiment parachuted behind enemy lines near Utah Beach in the 6 June Normandy invasion, with the objectives of assisting the 505th in securing the La Fière bridgehead and establishing a defensive line. Colonel George V. Millett, Jr. commanded the 507th at the time of the assault.

The regiment returned to England on 13 July and became attached to the 17th Airborne Division from 27 August 1944 until 1 March 1945, at which time it was permanently assigned to that division. The regiment was flown with its division in an emergency night-time airlift to France, from where it entered Belgium on 25 December 1944 and defended a line along the Meuse river. The 17th division attacked near Bastogne on 3 January 1945. On 14 January, the 507th took Bertogne, and on 6 February it crossed the Our river. Relieved by the 6th Armored Division, the 17th returned to France for reserve duty on 11 February 1945.

On 24 March 1945, the regiment parachuted with its division to assault east of the Rhine river. The next day the 507th, along with the 194th Glider Infantry, pressed across the Issel canal. Three days later the regiment seized Wulfen. The division advanced to relieve the 79th Infantry Division on 6 April 1945 along the Rhine-Herne canal. The 507th attacked across the canal two days later, and captured Essen on 10 April. After mopping up in the Ruhr area and receiving the surrender of Duisburg, the division took up military government duties until war's end. The 507th returned from Europe to Boston on 15 September 1945, and was inactivated the following day.

The regiment received the Presidential Unit Citation and the French Croix de Guerre with Palm for its conduct in Normandy. Its World War II campaigns were: Normandy, Rhineland, Ardennes-Alsace, and Central Europe.

507th PARACHUTE INFANTRY REGIMENT
(Colonel George V. Millett, Jr.)
  1st Battalion *(Lt Col Edwin J. Ostberg/Maj Ben F. Pearson)*
  2d Battalion *(Lt Col Charles J. Timmes)*
  3d Battalion *(Lt Col William H. Kuhn/Maj John T. Davis)*

508th Parachute Infantry Regiment

The 508th Parachute Infantry was constituted in the Army of the United States on 6 October 1942 and activated at Camp Blanding, Florida on 20 October 1942 under the Airborne Command. It was moved to Fort Benning, Georgia to commence jump school in Februay 1943, departed New York in December 1943, and arrived in the British Isles January 1944 to train for the Normandy invasion. The unit was attached to the 82d Airborne Division from 14 January 1944 to 20 January 1945 and from 24 January 1945 until the end of the war.

With only two practice night jumps behind them, the men of the 508th parachuted behind enemy lines at Utah beach on 6 June 1944. Their mission was to destroy two bridges over the Douve. After a widely scattered landing, the regiment assembled by 9 June under its commander, Colonel Roy E. Lindquist. In the ensuing days the 508th fought its way across the Douve river and into the town of Baupte, capturing Prétot at heavy cost on 20 June. The regiment sailed back to England on 13 July 1944.

The regiment parachuted with the 82d division south of Nijmegen, Holland on 17 September 1944 and fought there until 11 November. From its base camp in France, the 508th moved with the division to meet the Ardennes counteroffensive in Belgium on 18 December. The regiment parried German attacks on 25 and 28 December and fought a bloody battle for Thier-du-Mont ridge on 7 January 1945.

After a drive to the Siegfried Line, the regiment moved to the Roer River on 8 February to clear an area west of the river, and returned to France on 21 February. Starting 10 June 1945, the 508th infantry served as headquarters guards at Frankfurt. The regiment returned to New York on 24 November 1946 and was inactivated the following day.

In sum, the regiment's World War II campaigns included: Normandy, Rhineland, Ardennes-Alsace, and Central Europe. The 508th incurred 2,670 casualties in these campaigns. One man of the regiment received the Medal of Honor. The regiment received the Presidential Unit Citation and the French Croix de Guerre with Palm for its conduct in Normandy. Its coat of arms commemorates its actions in Normandy and Rhineland as well as its fourteen honors of World War II.

508th Parachute Infantry Regiment

508th PARACHUTE INFANTRY REGIMENT
(Colonel Roy E. Lindquist)
  1st Battalion *(Lt Col Herbert Batcheller/Maj Shields Warren, Jr.)*
  2d Battalion *(Col Thomas J.B. Shanley)*
  3d Battalion *(Lt Col Louis J. Mendez)*

325th Glider Infantry Regiment

The 325th Glider Infantry Regiment of World War II had its origins in the 325th Infantry constituted in the National Army on 5 August 1917 and organized 1 September 1917 as part of the 82d Division at Camp Gordon, Georgia. It was ordered into active service at Camp Claiborne, Louisiana on 25 March 1942. On 15 August 1942 it was redesignated the 325th Glider Infantry, assigned to the 82d Airborne Division, and moved to Fort Bragg, North Carolina. The 2d Battalion of the 401st Glider Infantry fought with the 3d Battalion of the 325th and was absorbed by it in April 1945. The 401st Infantry was constituted in 1918 as part of the 101st Division.

The regiment arrived in North Africa on 10 May 1943, and took part in the July invasion of Sicily. The 325th made an amphibious landing near Salerno, Italy on 15 September 1943.

In December 1943, the 82d Airborne moved to the British Isles to train for the Normandy invasion. Ninety men of the 325th came ashore on Utah Beach on 6 June 1944, with the bulk of the regiment gliding or sailing in the next day to help establish the la Fière bridgehead. It returned to England with the division on 13 July.

The regiment took part in the 17 September assault on Nijmegen-Arnhem, Holland, returning to France in November. The 325th was called into action in the Ardennes on 18 December 1944 and moved to Germany on 30 January 1945. It returned to France in February, and re-entered Germany on 2 April, where it remained through the end of hostilities and undertook occupation duties. The regiment returned to New York on 3 January 1946, and remained active until the end of 1946 at Fort Bragg, North Carolina.

One man of the regiment received the Medal of Honor for his conduct in Normandy. The entire regiment received the Presidential Unit Citation and the French Croix de Guerre with Palm for its conduct at Ste.-Mère-Église in Normandy. Its coat of arms commemorates: the regiment's origins in Georgia; its World War I service; its World War II actions in North Africa, Sicily, and Italy; its glider landings on Cherbourg peninsula and Nijmegen; and its breakthrough of the Siegfried Line. In sum, the World War II campaign streamers of the 325th are: Sicily, Naples-Foggia, Normandy, Rhineland, Ardennes-Alsace, and Central Europe.

325th Glider Infantry Regiment

325th GLIDER INFANTRY REGIMENT
(Colonel Harry L. Lewis)
  1st Battalion *(Lt Col R. Kleman Boyd)*
  2d Battalion *(Lt Col John H. Swenson)*
  3d Battalion *(Lt Col Charles A. Correll)*

THE BATTLES
505th Parachute Infantry Regiment

The 505th Parachute Infantry Regiment was to land east of the Merderet river and to proceed to capture Ste.-Mère-Église. In addition, the regiment was to capture river crossings near la Fière and Chef-du-Pont and to secure a defensive line running through Neuville-au-Plain and linking up with the 101st Airborne near Bandienville or Beuzeville-au-Plain. The regiment had one of the best D-Day drops with almost 1,000 of its 2,200 men landing where intended. Even those who missed the drop zone (DZ O) to the north and east managed to assemble rapidly. The regiment landed in an area empty of most defenders.

The 3d Battalion had the objective of capturing Ste.-Mère-Église and establishing roadblocks to the town's south and east. The battalion commander, Lieutenant Colonel Edward C. Krause, collected about one-quarter of his men and moved toward the town. Krause told his men to use only knives, bayonets, and grenades so that any small arms fire could be identified as enemy. Against little opposition the battalion occupied the town by 0430 and raised the same flag it had raised over Naples when it entered that city. By 0930 the town had been entirely cleared and the road blocks set up.

Meanwhile, Lieutenant Colonel Benjamin Vandervoort's 2d Battalion, which had suffered far greater dispersal than the 3d Battalion, had begun moving on its objective to establish a line through Neuville-au-Plain and Bandienville. Lacking information from Ste.-Mère-Église, the regimental commander ordered Vandervoort to go and capture that town. March and counter-march ensued until 0930 when regimental headquarters learned that a serious German counterattack against the town was under way.

About two German infantry companies supported by tanks and self-propelled guns attacked the southern roadblocks. The defenders were thin on the ground so Krause sent reinforcements. Around 1000 hours, Vandervoort's men also arrived to assist the defense. Although suffering a broken leg, Vandervoort continued in command using a hand-pulled cart as his headquarters. Before entering the town, Vandervoort had sent a platoon led by Lieutenant Turner B. Turnbull to Neuville-au-Plain. This proved fortuitous when the German drive against Ste.-Mère-Église expanded to approach from multiple directions.

In a classic small-unit action, Turnbull's 42 men conducted a fighting retreat that delayed the German advance from the north for eight hours. This bought time, at the cost of all but 16 of the defenders, for the balance of the two battalions to meet the German attack from the south. After repelling the first German thrust, Krause sent 80 men of Company I to strike the attacker's western flank. This effort hit a German truck convoy and destroyed it during a close range fight. The counterattack misled the Germans about the strength of the paratroop defense. Additional German efforts were tentative.

During the action at Ste.-Mère-Église, the regiment's 1st Battalion tried to secure the la Fière and Chef-du-Pont bridges from the east. Working in conjunction with units from its sister regiments who were advancing on the objective from the opposite bank, the battalion seemed on the verge of gaining its objective when command confusion struck. The culprits were three: the paratroopers who had landed on the far bank had been badly dispersed during their descent; the hedgerow countryside essentially penned small units into isolated fields of action making overall coordination difficult; and the Germans began a series of heavy counterattacks.

The counterattacks struck the forward defenses of the 1st Battalion around la Fière with heavy mortar and artillery fire. Two German tanks tried to cross to the east bank only to fall victim to a Company A roadblock. Up until 2000, the battalion was in dire straits. However, a decision made by assistant division commander Brigadier General James Gavin to leave a small force at Chef-du-Pont while the balance reinforced the 1st Battalion at la Fière paid dividends. Once the some 200 reinforcements arrived the eastern end of the la Fière position was secure.

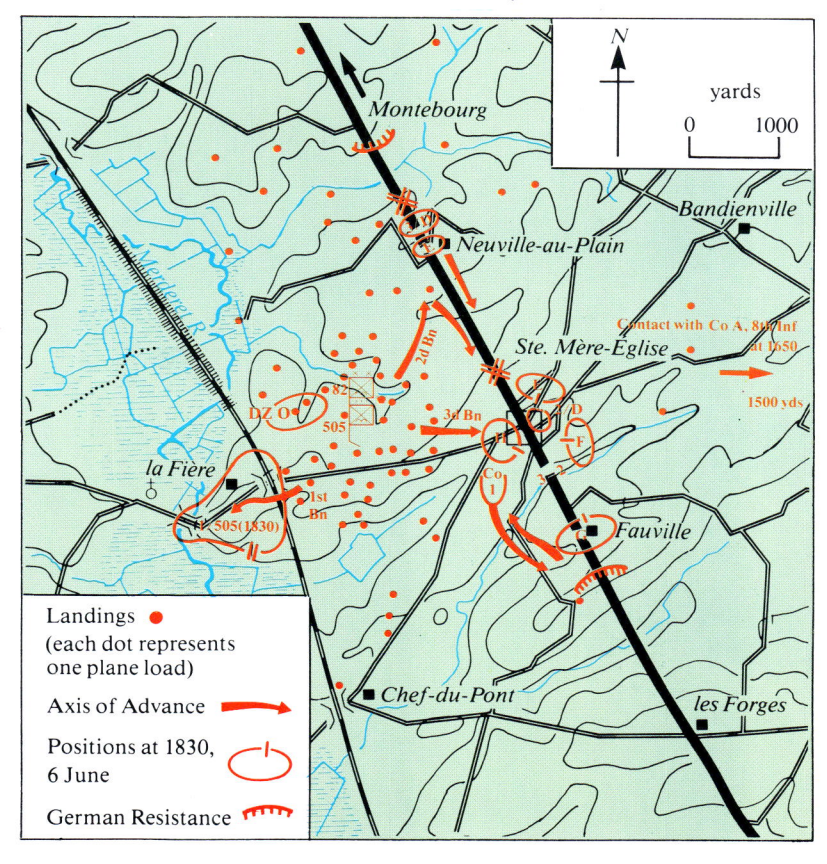

Above: **Dakotas over Ste. Mère - Église drop supplies to men of the 82d Airborne Division.**

THE BATTLES
505th Parachute Infantry Regiment

The 505th Parachute Infantry Regiment was to land east of the Merderet river and to proceed to capture Ste.-Mère-Église. In addition, the regiment was to capture river crossings near la Fière and Chef-du-Pont and to secure a defensive line running through Neuville-au-Plain and linking up with the 101st Airborne near Bandienville or Beuzeville-au-Plain. The regiment had one of the best D-Day drops with almost 1,000 of its 2,200 men landing where intended. Even those who missed the drop zone (DZ O) to the north and east managed to assemble rapidly. The regiment landed in an area empty of most defenders.

The 3d Battalion had the objective of capturing Ste.-Mère-Église and establishing roadblocks to the town's south and east. The battalion commander, Lieutenant Colonel Edward C. Krause, collected about one-quarter of his men and moved toward the town. Krause told his men to use only knives, bayonets, and grenades so that any small arms fire could be identified as enemy. Against little opposition the battalion occupied the town by 0430 and raised the same flag it had raised over Naples when it entered that city. By 0930 the town had been entirely cleared and the road blocks set up.

Meanwhile, Lieutenant Colonel Benjamin Vandervoort's 2d Battalion, which had suffered far greater dispersal than the 3d Battalion, had begun moving on its objective to establish a line through Neuville-au-Plain and Bandienville. Lacking information from Ste.-Mère-Église, the regimental commander ordered Vandervoort to go and capture that town. March and counter-march ensued until 0930 when regimental headquarters learned that a serious German counterattack against the town was under way.

About two German infantry companies supported by tanks and self-propelled guns attacked the southern roadblocks. The defenders were thin on the ground so Krause sent reinforcements. Around 1000 hours, Vandervoort's men also arrived to assist the defense. Although suffering a broken leg, Vandervoort continued in command using a hand-pulled cart as his headquarters. Before entering the town, Vandervoort had sent a platoon led by Lieutenant Turner B. Turnbull to Neuville-au-Plain. This proved fortuitous when the German drive against Ste.-Mère-Église expanded to approach from multiple directions.

In a classic small-unit action, Turnbull's 42 men conducted a fighting retreat that delayed the German advance from the north for eight hours. This bought time, at the cost of all but 16 of the defenders, for the balance of the two battalions to meet the German attack from the south. After repelling the first German thrust, Krause sent 80 men of Company I to strike the attacker's western flank. This effort hit a German truck convoy and destroyed it during a close range fight. The counterattack misled the Germans about the strength of the paratroop defense. Additional German efforts were tentative.

During the action at Ste.-Mère-Église, the regiment's 1st Battalion tried to secure the la Fière and Chef-du-Pont bridges from the east. Working in conjunction with units from its sister regiments who were advancing on the objective from the opposite bank, the battalion seemed on the verge of gaining its objective when command confusion struck. The culprits were three: the paratroopers who had landed on the far bank had been badly dispersed during their descent; the hedgerow countryside essentially penned small units into isolated fields of action making overall coordination difficult; and the Germans began a series of heavy counterattacks.

The counterattacks struck the forward defenses of the 1st Battalion around la Fière with heavy mortar and artillery fire. Two German tanks tried to cross to the east bank only to fall victim to a Company A roadblock. Up until 2000, the battalion was in dire straits. However, a decision made by assistant division commander Brigadier General James Gavin to leave a small force at Chef-du-Pont while the balance reinforced the 1st Battalion at la Fière paid dividends. Once the some 200 reinforcements arrived the eastern end of the la Fière position was secure.

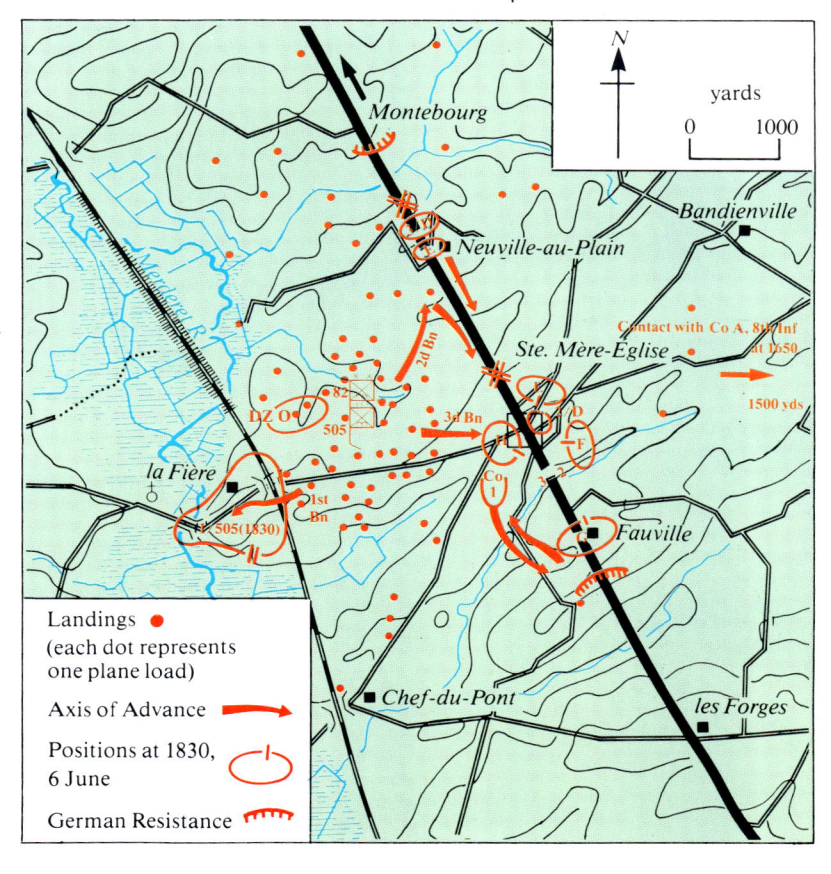

Above: **Dakotas over Ste.Mère-Église drop supplies to men of the 82d Airborne Division.**

THE BATTLES
507th Parachute Infantry Regiment

The 507th Parachute Infantry Regiment's mission was to screen the 505th's two bridgeheads over the Merderet at la Fière and Chef-du-Pont by pushing out a defensive line about three miles to the west. The regiment would defend the Douve river line and destroy the bridges at Pont l'Abbé and Beuzeville-la-Bastille to the West. Since these objectives were in the triangle at the confluence of the Merderet and Douve rivers, success depended heavily upon an accurate drop. When pathfinders were unable to mark the drop zone (DZ T) because of the presence of enemy soldiers, it caused transport pilots to overshoot and scatter many men into the flooded marshes along the Merderet. Aerial photos had indicated that the river was narrow and bordered by a grassy swamp. These photos were deceptive and did not reveal that the grass had grown thickly atop a swamp several feet deep. When heavily laden paratroopers landed here, it proved very difficult for them to extricate themselves. Much valuable, and heavy, equipment sank in the swamp. Among many, General James Gavin spent hours in fruitless labor trying to extricate a jeep and anti-tank gun from the marshes. A railroad embankment leading to la Fière was one of the few identifiable terrain features. Many men used it as a landmark and it caused groups from a variety of units to converge on la Fière.

Captain F.V. Schwartzwalder landed in the swamp east of the Merderet (the opposite bank from the intended drop zone), located the embankment, and moved toward la Fière collecting paratroopers as he went. Here he encountered enemy defenders and was unable to rush the village. Colonel Roy Lindquist, a 508th officer, had a similar experience. He led a mixed group of men from both the 507th and 508th along the embankment and was joined by 30 men of the 507th commanded by Lieutenant John H. Wisner. Men continued to drift in, building up this force to between 500 and 600 men. Later in the day these men, including Company G, 507th Parachute Infantry would work across the bridge and causeway from la Fière.

The regiment's 2d Battalion, commanded by Lieutenant Colonel Charles J. Timmes, landed close to their designated drop zone 1,000 yards east of Amfreville. Timmes quickly assembled 50 men and sent out a patrol towards the west end of la Fière causeway. This force could not make progress although ten men did manage to establish a machine gun in the Cauquigny church that dominated the causeway's western end.

When the causeway had been cleared from the east side, Schwartzwalder and his 70 some men crossed and headed for their objective to the west. Due to a command confusion, the 505th did not secure the causeway behind them. Only four officers, including Lieutenant Lewis Levy of Company D and eight enlisted men of the 507th, guarded the bridge when a German counterattack struck. Levy and his men defended their position with one machine gun, rifles, and grenades and even managed to disable two German tanks with Gammon grenades. Finally they had to withdraw northward leaving the causeway's western end in German hands. This isolated Timmes and Schwartzwalder from units in la Fière. Timmes had his men assume a defensive position in an orchard near Amfreville. German attacks bumped into their perimeter and surged past toward la Fière. This force would remain out of contact for two more days.

The regimental commander, Colonel George V. Millet, Jr., landed west of Amfreville. Although he was less than 1,000 yards from Timmes and his 2d Battalion group, Millet did not know this. Collecting some 75 men, with no contact with other friendly forces, Millet fought a lonely battle until D+4. Other scattered groups likewise fought independent actions on D-Day and thereafter. Although the dispersed drop contributed to German misapprehension regarding American intentions, it also meant that many of the groups would succumb to overwhelming German pressure before they could link up with friendly forces.

By noon of 8 June, the 82d Airborne Division would report that it still had managed to collect only 2,100 effectives, fewer than one third of its authorized strength.

THE BATTLES
508th Parachute Infantry Regiment

The two regiments assigned the mission of securing the West bank of the Merderet river in the triangle at the confluence of the Merderet and Douve rivers depended heavily upon an accurate drop. Because of the presence of German infantry, the pathfinders were unable to mark the respective drop zones (DZ N north of Picauville and DZ T north of Amreville) and therefore both the 508th and the 507th experienced a dispersed landing. To add to the problem, what had appeared in reconnaissance photographs as solid pasture land bordering the river turned out to be marshy water meadows. Many of the paratroopers, carrying weapons, ammunition and other heavy equipment found themselves landing in a virtual swamp. Even when the men succeeded in extricating themselves, losing much of their heavy weapons in the marsh, it was difficult for them to concentrate their forces and orientate towards their objectives. However the railroad embankment running through la Fière on the east bank of the Merderet did provide a landmark and groups from a variety of units made their way towards this feature.

Colonel Roy Lindquist, the commander of the 508th Parachute Infantry, landed in the swamps northeast of Amfreville and moved toward the rail embankment. He assembled about 100 men as he moved along. He decided to use the embankment to move to la Fière and thence continue on to his objective at Pont l'Abbé. German machine gun fire prevented the use of the la Fière bridge. General Gavin, who had appeared on the scene, ordered Lindquist to assume command of a mixed force of 400 men. After Gavin departed to try to find a crossing at Chef-du-Pont, divisional commander Ridgway appeared on the scene and ordered Lindquist to capture the bridge. At noon, Lindquist led his men in an attack over the exposed and narrow causeway. It managed to link up with a patrol of the 2d Battalion, 507th Parachute Infantry Regiment that was moving on the bridge from the opposite direction. However, command confusion caused the Americans to relinquish the bridge. Then, a heavy German counterattack struck Company B which had moved to the bridge's western end. Unable to hold its ground, the company's survivors had to swim back to the east bank under heavy German fire.

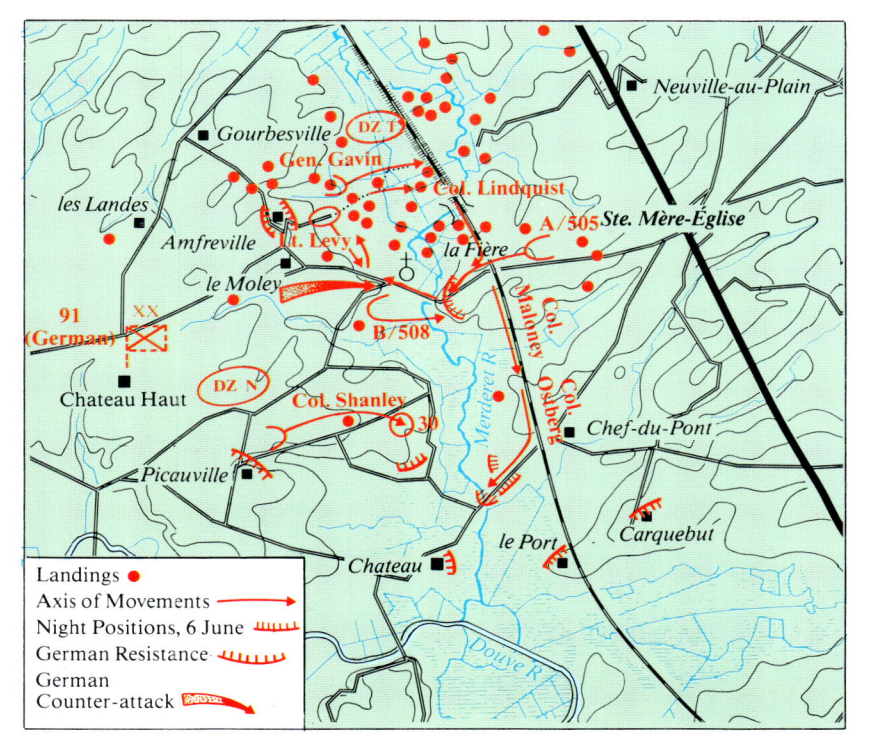

The largest regimental force to assemble west of the Merderet was led by the 2d Battalion's Colonel Thomas J.B. Shanley. Shanley landed near Picauville and assembed a small force. Lacking the strength to proceed to Pont l'Abbé, his battalion objective, Shanley moved to the northeast to join a force of about 60 men. During this movement he was joined by another patrol. However, random enemy pressure forced Shanley's group to engage until mid-afternoon. Although Shanley did not know it, he confronted major elements of the German 1057th Regiment that had orders to wipe out American paratroopers west of the river. Deciding that an advance against the dug-in German forces around Pont l'Abbé could not succeed, Shanley led his group toward the regimental assembly area on the high ground of Hill 30. Three enlisted men, Corporal Ernest T. Robertrs, Private Otto K. Zwingman, and Private John A. Lockwood, performed gallantly by holding an outpost for two hours in order to cover the movement of the balance of the unit. Their sacrificial rearguard (all three were captured) earned them the Distinguished Service Cross. Shanley reached the high ground around 2300 and formed his men into an all around defensive perimeter that dominated the Chef-du-Pont causeway. Shanley's fight helped deflect enemy pressure against the defenders at la Fière and Chef-du-Pont, and in the coming days would contribute substantially to establishing a bridgehead over the Merderet.

So scattered were most of the other elements of the 508th that dropped west of the river that they did not coalesce into an effective fighting force on D-Day. Instead, they fought individual and small group actions for their survival. By the end of D-Day the division reported it controlled only 40 percent of its combat infantry and 10 percent of its artillery. The majority were feared lost, although in fact they were merely unable to gain the assembly areas. For example, some elements did not manage to rejoin the 508th until five days after D-Day.

US 101st Airborne Division

The 101st Airborne Division was activated at Camp Claiborne, Louisiana on 16 August 1942 under command of Major General William C. Lee and transferred to Fort Bragg, North Carolina in September. It was one of two airborne divisions created by dividing up the 82d Infantry Division. General Lee said of the division: "The 101st Airborne . . . has no history, but it has a rendezvous with destiny . . ."

General Lee had played an early role in American airborne history. After serving in France in World War I as a platoon leader and a company commander, he taught military science and became an expert in tank warfare. As a major in the Office of the Chief of Infantry, Lee worked on the development of the infantryman as a paratrooper, studying the methods of the U.S. Forest Service fire-jumpers.

A test platoon was formed from infantry volunteers in July 1940, and they made their first jump on 16 August. Some of the battalion combat leaders in the 101st at Normandy served in the battalion that grew out of this test platoon, including: Robert F. Sink, Julian Ewell, Patrick J. Cassidy, Robert G. Cole, as well as Robert L. Strayer who became a regimental commander. As a colonel, Lee assumed leadership of the Airborne Command at Fort Bragg on 21 March 1942. As a general, he established the Parachute School at Fort Benning, Georgia in May.

The 101st Airborne Division in its initial form comprised: Headquarters, the 502d Parachute Infantry, the 327th and 401st Glider Infantries, the divisional artillery, the 377th Parachute Field Artillery Battalion, the 321st and 907th Glider Field Artillery Battalions, the 101st Airborne Signal Company, 326th Airborne Engineer Battalion, 426th Airborne Quartermaster Company and the 326th Airborne Medical Company. By 1944 the division had added the 81st Airborne Anti-aircraft Battalion and several auxiliary companies and platoons, as well as combat attachments comprising three more entire tank and tank destroyer battalions.

The 101st Airborne sailed to England in September 1943 where they took part in training exercises and practice jumps for their first combat of the war. When General Lee suffered a heart attack, the division passed to the command of Major General Maxwell D. Taylor in March 1944.

On 6 June 1944, the 101st shared in the air and sea assault of Normandy. In the predawn hours, the 502d Parachute Infantry Regiment and the attached 501st and 506th Parachute Infantry Regiments parachuted behind enemy lines, while supporting divisional units arrived by sea and gliders brought in equipment and troops. The division played a key role in the capture of Carentan. The 101st returned to England on 13 July for rehabilitation. Airborne leaders were eager to stage another major operation. However, such was the speed of the allied pursuit across France and Belgium that no sooner had an operation been prepared than the ground forces had already overrun the proposed landing zones. Then came Arnhem, the proverbial "bridge too far". The 101st air assaulted Nijmegen-Arnhem, Holland on 17 September 1944. It took the Veghel and Zon bridges, as well as Eindhoven, Zon, St. Oedenrode, Veghel, and Schijndel. On 28 November, the division was relieved and returned to France.

The division returned to action in the Ardennes on 18 December 1944 under the temporary command of Brigadier General Anthony McAuliffe. Its epic defense of surrounded and besieged Bastogne won the entire division the Distinguished Unit Citation. When the Germans demanded surrender on 22 December, General McAuliffe replied with the now legendary, "Nuts!" The general later said of his men: "With the type of soldier I had under my command, possessing such fighting spirit, all that I had to do was to make a few basic decisions – my men did the rest."

On 25 February 1945, the 101st retired to France for rehabilitation. In late March, the division moved out to hold the Ruhr pocket, from where they sent periodic patrols across the Rhine. It took up military government duties while advancing across southern Germany into Bavaria. Ordered to march on Berchtesgaden on 4 May, the division suffered its last three battle casualties en route as the war came to an end. After a period of occupation in southern Germany and Austria, the "Screaming Eagles" returned to France on 1 August 1945. The division was inactivated in France on 30 November.

During the course of hostilities the division lost 1,766 killed and 6,388 wounded, of whom 324 later died of their wounds. Two men of the division, from the 502d Parachute Infantry Regiment, won the Medal of Honor, one of which was for the invasion of Normandy. In sum, the 101st participated in the World War II campaigns of Normandy, Rhineland, Ardennes-Alsace, and Central Europe.

Major General Maxwell Taylor was West Point educated and entered the Corps of Engineers in 1922. He transferred to the field artillery in 1926. In 1942, as chief of staff of the 82d Division, Taylor helped organize the division's conversion to the airborne service. The next year he went overseas as 82d Airborne Division artillery commander and fought through the Sicilian and Italian campaigns. He received command of the 101st in March 1944.

US 101st AIRBORNE DIVISION
(Major General Maxwell D. Taylor)

501st Parachute Infantry Regiment
(Colonel Howard R. Johnson)

502d Parachute Infantry Regiment
(Colonel George V.H. Moseley, Jr.)

506th Parachute Infantry Regiment
(Colonel Robert F. Sink)

327th Glider Infantry Regiment
(Colonel George S. Wear)

377th Parachute Field Artillery Battalion

501st Parachute Infantry Regiment

The 501st Parachute Infantry Regiment was constituted 24 February 1942 in the Army of the United States, activated at Camp Toccoa, Georgia on 15 November 1942, assigned to the Airborne Command a month later, and moved to Fort Benning, Georgia in March 1943. The 501st Parachute Battalion, which had been activated in October 1940 at Fort Benning, became the regiment's 1st Battalion. The regiment was assigned to the 2d Airborne Brigade in September 1943 and sailed to England January 1944, where it was attached to the 101st Airborne Division in May 1944.

Under command of Colonel Howard R. Johnson (who made more than 100 career parachute jumps before his death in action in Holland), the 501st parachuted behind enemy lines at Utah Beach on 6 June 1944 with the mission of capturing the la Barquette locks on the Douve river. Along with the 506th Infantry, the regiment captured an entire enemy battalion on the day after D-Day. The regiment returned to England on 13 July 1944 with its division.

On 17 September 1944, the regiment participated in the air assault on Nijmegen-Arnhem. The 501st captured Eerde, then advanced on Heeswijk, taking 418 prisoners in the process. With Dutch citizens providing information on enemy positions, the regiment took Schijndel and Veghel on 21-22 September. In October the 501st sent out a patrol on a daring mission into enemy territory. They were covertly to observe German movements, capture an enemy vehicle and prisoners, and drive them back to their base. The six-man patrol returned with 32 prisoners.

The regiment moved to France in November, and returned to action in the Ardennes on 18 December 1944. The 101st Airborne's epic defense of Bastogne is well-known. The 501st moved into Germany on 4 April 1945 and remained there until inactivated on 20 August 1945.

The regiment's coat of arms commemorates its role in the liberation of Veghel, Holland and its combat at Bastogne, Belgium. Its motto, "Geronimo," was first heard during the initial jump of the regiment's test platoon and has been in use ever since.

The full regiment received Presidential Unit Citations for its conduct in Normandy and Bastogne and the French Croix de Guerre with Palm for its conduct in Normandy.

501st Parachute Infantry Regiment

501st PARACHUTE INFANTRY REGIMENT
(Colonel Howard R. Johnson)
 1st Battalion *(Lt Col Robert C. Carroll/Maj Harry W. Kinnard)*
 2d Battalion *(Lt Col Robert A. Ballard)*
 3d Battalion *(Lt Col Julian J. Ewell)*

502d Parachute Infantry Regiment

The 502d Parachute Infantry Regiment was constituted in the Army of the United States on 24 February 1942 and activated at Fort Benning, Georgia on 2 March 1942. On 15 August 1942 it was assigned to the 101st Airborne Division, and on 24 September, moved to Fort Bragg, North Carolina. The regiment sailed to England in September 1943.

On 6 June 1944, the 502d parachuted behind enemy lines at Utah Beach, under the command of Colonel George V.H. Moseley, Jr., with the mission of securing the two northern beach exits. The 502d played a key role in the heavy fighting for Carentan from 8-11 June. The division moved to Cherbourg on 30 June, and returned to England on 13 July.

In the 101st Airborne's aerial assault on Nijmegen-Arnhem on 17 September 1944, the 502d took St. Oedenrode and Best, the latter after heavy losses. A detachment from the 502d was captured during the fight for Best, but broke free and in turn seized their captors.

The 101st withdrew to France in late November, and then returned to action in the Ardennes on 18 December. Its epic defense of surrounded Bastogne is well-known. On Christmas morning, German tanks attacked the 502d and 327th Infantries at Champs. Despite the surprise of the attack, seven German tanks were destroyed with little loss to the regiment.

The 101st moved into Germany on 4 April 1945, serving in the Ruhr pocket, the Memmingen area, and near Miesbach before war's end. The 502d undertook military government duties in the rear areas and assumed responsibility for displaced person camps near München-Gladbach. The regiment was inactivated with the rest of its division in France on 30 November 1945.

The full regiment received Presidential Unit Citations for its conduct in Normandy and Bastogne, and the French Croix de Guerre with Palm for its conduct in Normandy. Two men of the 502d were awarded the Medal of Honor, one of them for his conduct in Normandy. The regiment's coat of arms commemorates its bayonet charge at Carentan, Normandy, its role in the liberation of Best, Holland, and its combat in Bastogne, Belgium. In sum, the World War II campaigns of the 502d were: Normandy, Rhineland, Ardennes-Alsace, annd Central Europe.

502d Parachute Infantry Regiment

502d PARACHUTE INFANTRY REGIMENT
(Colonel George V.H. Moseley, Jr.)
 1st Battalion *(Lt Col Patrick F. Cassidy)*
 2d Battalion *(Lt Col Steve A. Chappuis)*
 3d Battalion *(Lt Col Robert G. Cole)*

506th Parachute Infantry Regiment

The 506th Parachute Infantry Regiment was constituted in the Army of the United States on 1 July 1942, activated at Camp Toccoa, Georgia on 20 July 1942, and moved to Fort Benning in December, at which time it was attached to the Airborne Command. The regiment was attached to the 101st Airborne Division from 1 June 1943 to 1 March 1945, and permanently assigned to the division thereafter. Following several relocations within the U.S., the 506th sailed to England in September 1943. Colonel Robert F. Sink commanded the regiment through all of its World War II campaigns.

On 6 June 1944, the 506th parachuted behind enemy lines at Utah Beach with the objectives of capturing two bridges over the Douve river and seizing an area containing two beach exits. In the ensuing days, the 506th shared in the capture of an entire German battalion, took Vierville, captured Carentan, and parried an attempt to retake the town. The regiment returned to England on 13 July with its division.

506th Parachute Infantry Regiment

The 506th shared in the 101st Airborne's assault of Nijmegen-Arnhem on 17 September 1944. On 23 September, the regiment reopened the Veghel-Uden highway, and drove the enemy from the Koevering roadblock two days later. The division moved to France for rehabilitation in late November.

The division returned to action at Bastogne on 18 December 1944. Its epic defense of the surrounded town is well-known. On 9 January 1945, the 506th moved on Recogne, and several days later seized Foy-Notre-Dame, and then Neville and Rachamps.

The division relieved the 97th Infantry Division in Germany on 4 April 1945. A patrol from the 506th conducted a raid across the Rhine on 11-12 April. The 506th was inactivated along with the rest of the 101st Airborne in France on 30 November 1945.

The regiment's coat of arms recalls its Georgia origins, its two air-assaults, its capture of Eindhoven, Holland, and its defense of Bastogne. The full regiment received Presidential Unit Citations for its conduct in Normandy and Bastogne, and the French Croix de Guerre with Palm for its conduct in Normandy. In sum, the World War II campaigns of the 506th infantry are: Normandy, Rhineland, Ardennes-Alsace, and Central Europe.

506th PARACHUTE INFANTRY REGIMENT
(Colonel Robert F. Sink)
  1st Battalion *(Lt Col William L. Turner)*
  2d Battalion *(Lt Col Robert L. Strayer)*
  3d Battalion *(Lt Col Robert L. Wolverton)*

327th Glider Infantry Regiment

The 327th Glider Infantry Regiment of World War II originated as the 327th Infantry of the 82d Division on 17 September 1917 at Camp Gordon, Georgia. It was recalled from reserve at Camp Claiborne, Louisiana on 25 March 1942. On 15 August 1942, it was redesignated the 327th Glider Infantry Regiment and assigned to the 101st Airborne Division, and moved to Fort Bragg, North Carolina in September. The 1st Battalion of the 401st Glider Infantry fought with the 3d Battalion of the 327th and was absorbed by it in April 1945. The 401st Infantry was constituted in 1918 as part of the 101st Division. While paratroopers were volunteers who received extra pay, the glidermen were assigned to their high-risk unit and did not receive any extra pay. It was not until 1944 that glidermen began to draw flight pay.

The regiment sailed to England in September 1943. Under the command of Colonel George S.

327th Glider Infantry Regiment

Wear, the 327th made both amphibious and glider landings on Utah Beach on 6 June 1944. In the ensuing days, the glider infantry reinforced parachute regiments on the Carentan causeway, relieved them at la Barquette and le Port, and moved on Carentan. The 327th returned to England with its division on 13 July.

The 327th participated in the 17 September 1944 air assault on Nijmegen-Arnhem, protecting the landing zone and the glider-borne supplies as well as fighting at Veghel and Opheusden. The division was relieved and returned to France on 25 November, but was soon recalled to action in the Ardennes. On 10 December the 101st moved to Bastogne, which it held under siege in one of the legendary episodes of the war. After another period in France, the division advanced into Germany on 4 April 1945, reaching Berchtesgaden by war's end. The regiment was inactivated along with the rest of the division in France on 30 November 1945.

The regiment's coat of arms recalls its World War I service, its glider landings in Normandy and Holland, and its combat at Bastogne. The regiment received the French Croix de Guerre with Palm for its conduct in Normandy. In sum, the World War II campaigns of the 327th Glider Infantry were: Normandy, Rhineland, Ardennes-Alsace, and Central Europe.

327th GLIDER INFANTRY REGIMENT
(Colonel George S. Wear)
  1st Battalion *(Lt Col Hartford F. Salee)*
  2d Battalion *(Lt Col Thomas J. Rouzie)*
  3d Battalion *(Lt Col Ray C. Allen)*

THE BATTLES
501st Parachute Infantry Regiment

The 501st Parachute Infantry's 1st Battalion had the mission to capture the lock on the Douve River at la Barquette. This lock controlled the river's water level to the west as far as the confluence of the Merderet. In German hands it could provide an important obstacle to the breakout from Utah Beach. The 2d Battalion would blow the Douve bridges on the main road from St. Come-du-Mont to Carentan. If possible, the regiment would take St. Come-du-Mont and destroy the rail bridge to the west.

The regiment was badly dispersed during its drop. Particularly hard hit were members of the 1st Battalion command group. However, the regiment's commander, Colonel Howard R. Johnson, landed squarely in the middle of the planned drop zone. Moving toward his objective, Johnson collected some 140 miscellaneous men. Sending 50 men ahead to overrun the lock, Johnson placed the balance of his force in defensive positions near the lock. After securing this prime objective, Johnson sent combat patrols toward the bridges 2,000 yards away. This effort drew heavy German fire and decided the colonel to limit himself to holding the lock while trying to move north to make contact with elements of his regiment at Bse. Addeville.

Johnson took about 50 men toward this village in hopes of collecting enough strength to continue against St. Come-du-Mont. Arriving at Bse. Addeville around 0900, Johnson found that his regimental S-3 Major R.J. Allen, had collected a mere 100 miscellaneous men and that they were already engaged with Germans to the north and west. Johnson was puzzled as to how to proceed given the paucity of strength.

Later in the morning, having heard the reassuring news broadcast by the BBC that the invasion "is going according to plan", Johnson decided to proceed with the regional mission. Leaving a small force at Bse. Addeville, he returned to the lock in preparation for an advance against the bridges. Then he learned that some 250 men of his 2d Battalion, led by Colonel Bullard, were heavily engaged some 1,000 yards to the northwest. He badly wanted these men to join his own command to give him the strength to attack the bridges. The problem was that German forces interposed between the two American units. While Johnson led a relief force toward Bullard, heavy German pressure built up against the paratroop force defending the lock. Fortunately, a naval shore fire control officer managed to direct remarkably accurate fire from the cruiser Quincy against the German position. Emboldened by this success, Johnson tried again to take the Douve bridges. Again heavy German fire thwarted this effort. He lacked the manpower to accomplish his secondary missions.

While the action around the lock was taking place, the 2d Battalion had assembled between Angouville-au-Plain and les Droueries. Colonel Ballard tried to move toward the lock but encountered stiff resistance. Persistent efforts to force through to maneuver around the German position at les Droueries failed in the face of small arms and mortar fire.

On D-Day, the 501st Parachute Infantry managed to capture its prime objective, the lock at la Barquette. However, strong resistance kept it from seizing St. Come-du-Mont and destroying the rail and highway bridges north of Carentan.

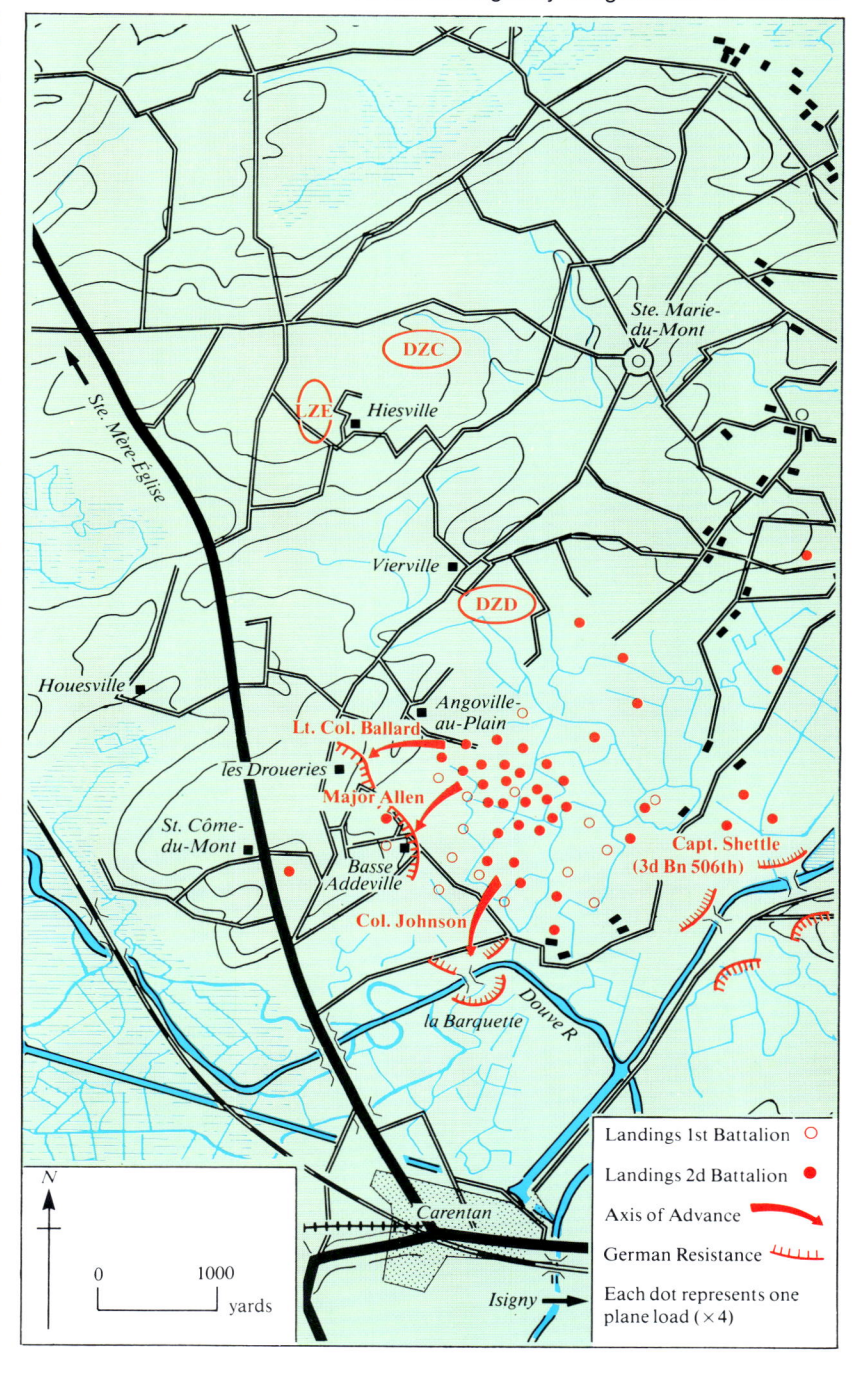

THE BATTLES
502d Parachute Infantry Regiment

The 502d Parachute Infantry, supported by the 377th Parachute Field Artillery Battalion, was to drop immediately to the west of Exits 3 and 4 between Foucarville and St.-Martin-de-Varreville. Their drop zone (DZ A) was just behind Utah Beach. The 2d Battalion had the mission of destroying the coastal battery at St.-Martin-de-Varreville supported by the 3d Battalion if necessary. While the 2d Battalion remained at the battery in regimental reserve and established connection with the 506th Parachute Infantry, the 3d Battalion would secure the beach exits to allow the 4th Division to move inland along the causeway over the flooded ground. The 1st Battalion was to capture a group of buildings in the small hamlet of Mésières which was believed to serve as quarters for the artillery crew. The drop was to take place in four serials staged at ten-minute intervals: 2d Battalion with regimental headquarters; 3d Battalion; 1st Battalion; and artillery.

In the event, the 2d Battalion missed its drop zone entirely. Landing on unfamiliar ground far from the designated assembly points, it spent most of D-Day trying to reassemble.

Lieutenant Colonel Robert G. Cole, commander of the 3d Battalion, landed several hundred yards east of Ste.-Mére-Église. Unable to orient himself he began moving toward that village, all the while collecting men from a variety of outfits including a few from the 82d Airborne. Once Cole realized where he was, he backtracked toward the beach exits. His party, now grown to about 75 men, encountered a small German convoy and killed several enemy soldiers while capturing 10 prisoners. Cole sent a recon group toward St.- Martin-de-Varreville and the coastal battery. They found the position had been destroyed by bombing. Cole split his men into two groups with one each assigned to Exits 3 and 4. Around 0930 German soldiers began retreating toward his position (and away from the pressure on the beach). Without loss to the paratroopers, Cole's unit killed 50 to 75 fleeing enemy. By 1300 he had established contact with the 1st Battalion of 8th Infantry.

The 1st Battalion experienced the regiment's most difficult fight on D-Day. Battalion commander Lieutenant Colonel Patrick J. Cassidy landed in the middle of his unit's drop zone. Collecting men and getting oriented, Cassidy began moving toward the artillery garrison.

Cassidy planned to establish a blocking position at the St. Martin-de-Varreville intersection to prevent any German movement from the east toward Utah beach, and then to clear the artillery barracks. After scouting the beach exits, Cassidy sent 45 men to Foucarville to anchor the right of the battalion's position. Shortly after noon, this force trapped and destroyed a four-vehicle German troop convoy. A sizeable German force sat atop a dominating hill overlooking the paratrooper's roadblock. But they proved unaggressive. Just before midnight, bluffed into overestimating the American strength by the heavy volume of mortar and machine gun fire, the Germans surrendered. They, in turn, had captured about 50 paratroop prisoners. The released prisoners took up arms and shot down some 50 Germans who chose to run instead of to surrender. A total of 87 Germans surrendered to the paratroopers.

Meanwhile a sergeant conducted the attack against the artillery quarters. A stiff fight ensued. Finally, at 1530, bazooka rounds set afire the roof of the last defended building and more than 100 Germans were killed or captured as they tried to flee. The capture of this objective and the arrival of the regimental commander with some 200 men allowed Cassidy the freedom to move on to the north to defend the regiment's flank. He split his force into three combat patrols and all of them became engaged in battles in the twilight.

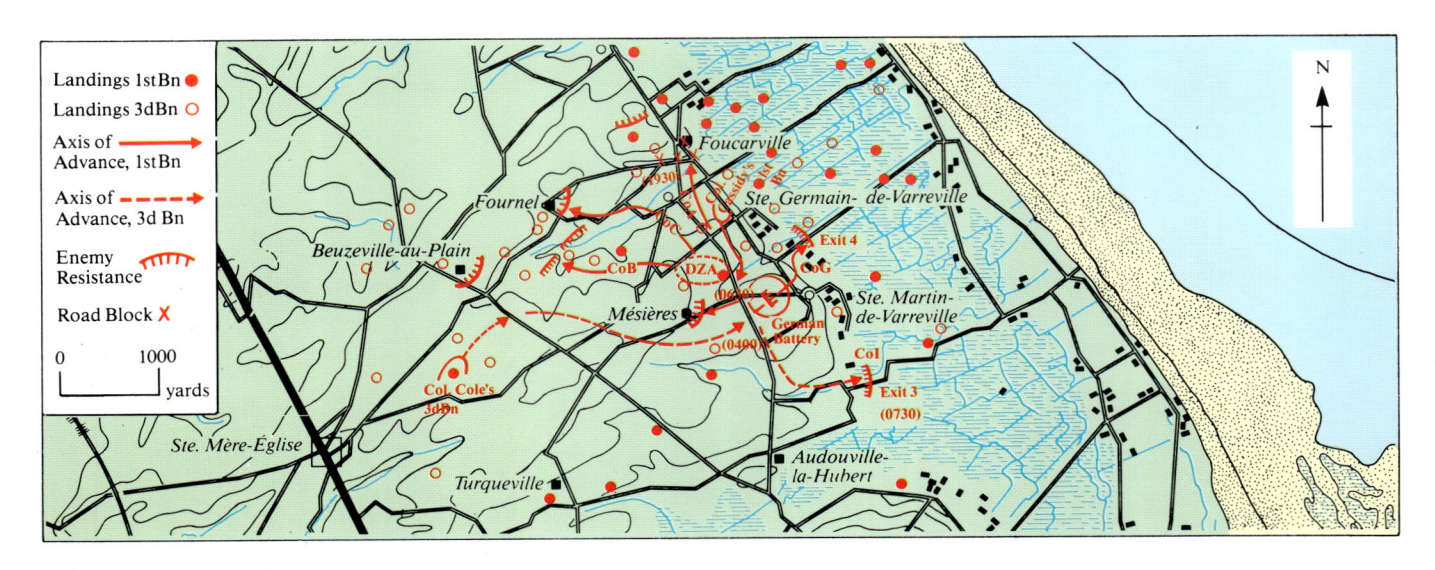

THE BATTLES
506th Parachute Infantry Regiment

Colonel Robert L. Sink and his regimental headquarters along with the 1st and 2d Battalions of the 506th Parachute Infantry were to land between Hiesville and Ste. Marie-du-Mont on DZ C. The 3d Battalion and a platoon of the 326th Engineer Battalion joined by two demolition sections were to land between Vierville and Bse. Addeville. The regiment had a twofold mission. It was to capture the western edge of the flooded area behind Utah Beach between Audouville-la-Hubert and Pouppeville. It was also to defend the Douve river line and capture two bridges near the mouth of the Douve as a stepping stone for future offensive actions. The demolition teams were to prepare the bridges for destruction just in case.

When the regiment's transport aircraft neared the French coast, fog and German flak caused the flying formation to disperse. Consequently, the regiment experienced a widely scattered drop. For example, of 81 planes scheduled to drop men in one zone, only 10 found the mark.

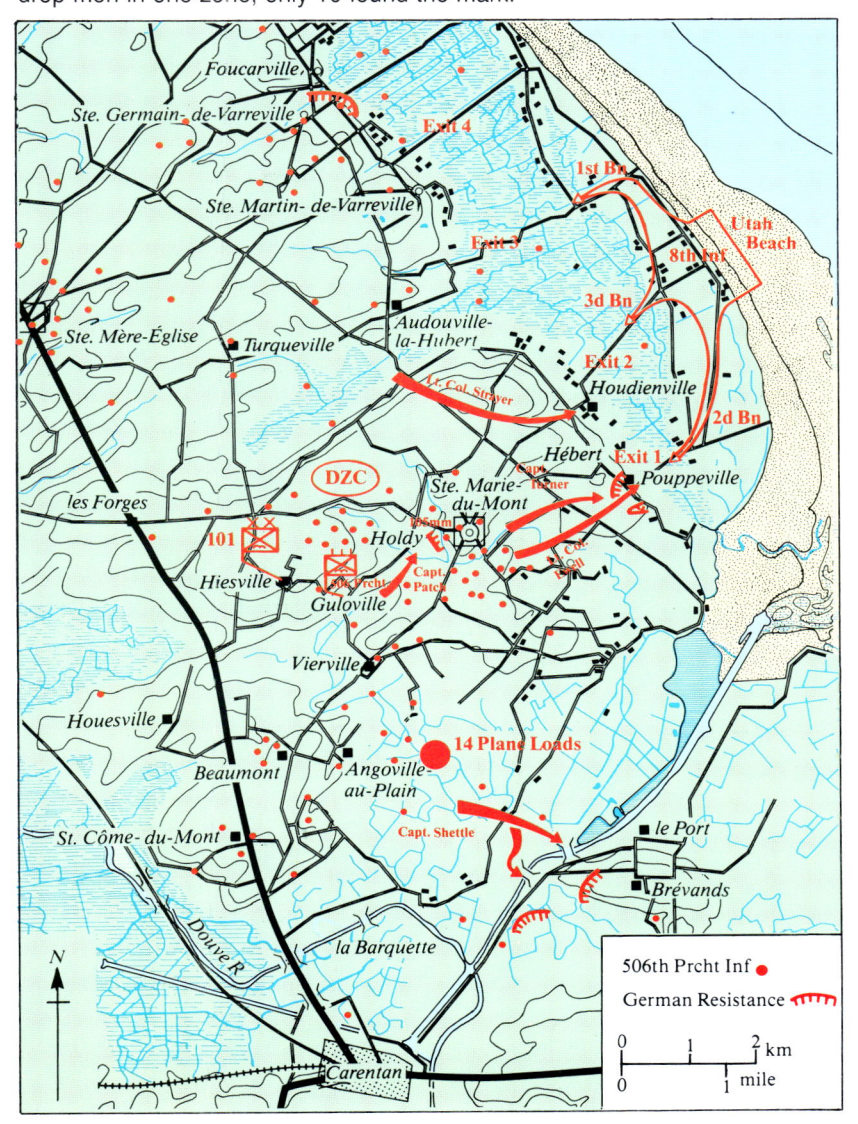

Nonetheless, Colonel Sink managed to collect 40 men from his headquarters unit within two hours of landing. Along with fifty 1st Battalion men gathered by their leader, Lieutenant Colonel William L. Turner, the group moved toward the key beach exits. Rather than split the command, Sink sent Turner to occupy Pouppeville and seize Exit 1. This group had to engage in several small fights and by the time it reached Pouppeville it found the village in the hands of elements of the 501st Parachute Infantry.

Meanwhile, unbeknownst to Sink, his 2d Battalion, commanded by Lieutenant Colonel Robert L. Strayer, was moving on Exit 2. Although dropped entirely outside of their zone, 200 men of Strayer's unit managed to assemble rapidly. Along with some 20 men of the 508th Parachute Infantry, this group encountered a moving German column around 0430. For most of the morning German machine gun fire pinned Strayer's men. Finally, part of Company D managed to bypass the resistance nest and reach Exit 2 by 1330. About an hour later the balance of Strayer's unit joined them. By 1800, after the 4th Division infantry and tanks had passed, the unit assembled at Houdienville.

During most of the day Sink had no idea where his 2d and 3d Battalions were and only limited information about the enemy. At Holdy, some 1,000 yards northeast of his command post, 70 of his men found a previously unsuspected enemy 105mm battery. Initially the defenders repelled all attacks. When Sink sent in another 70 or so men from his 1st Battalion, the Germans withdrew behind the earth revetments of their battery position. Bazooka fire softened this position and then the paratroopers stormed the battery. Leaving some men to garrison the battery site, Captain Lloyd E. Patch pressed on with a small group to attack Ste. Marie-du-Mont from the west. Simultaneously, elements of the 4th Infantry Division advanced against the village's eastern face and the village fell. Confused fighting continued around Sink's command post for most of the day. Twice Sink had to commit his entire headquarters group to repel German attacks.

Unknown to Sink, a platoon-size force of 3d Battalion men assembled and moved to the northern bridge at le Port around 0430. Captain Charles G. Shettle led this force across the bridge and went for the second bridge as well. For two hours an uneven fight raged. Superior German numbers forced Shettle to recross the bridge and defend the west bank for the remainder of the day. Shettle had thus established an anchor point on the 101st Division's south flank. With this, in spite of a day of extraordinary confusion, the regiment had almost managed to accomplish its D-Day missions.

29

THE BATTLES
327th Glider Infantry Regiment

At the beginning of World War II, when intrepid German glidermen demonstrated the glider's potential to deliver a surprise assault against Fort Eban Emael, the military world took notice. When developing airborne operations for the cross-channel attack, American planners included a prominent role for the glidermen. The 434th and 437th Troop Carrier Groups were chosen for special training to fly the transports that would tow the gliders. The glider pilots themselves had both to learn to fly their gliders and to undergo ground combat training, since once they landed they would serve as infantry. The assault would utilize both American-built Wacos and the larger British Horsas. These latter were needed to deliver the 57mm anti-tank guns and the 105mm airborne howitzers. The Wacos had steel tubing frames that provided pilot and crew some minimal crash protection while the all wood Horsas had no such protection.

Natural and man-made obstacles would interfere with glider landings. The hedgerow country, with its small, compartmentalized fields, offered difficult landing zones. At the urging of General feldmarschall Erwin Rommel, German soldiers and conscripted French workers had labored to sow all open fields with Rommel's "asparagus", eight to twelve foot long wooden poles designed to impale gliders.

Two glider landing missions were scheduled to support the 101st Airborne on D-Day. The first, code-named 'Chicago', would land at 0400, three hours after the first paratroops had dropped. Led by the assistant divisional commander, Brigadier General Pratt, this landing would reinforce the division with glidermen of the 327th Glider Infantry Regiment and deliver anti-tank guns and ammunition. The second mission, code-named 'Keokuk', would take place at 2100. It would be the allies' first daylight (in Normandy true darkness would not occur until two hours later) glider landing. The balance of the division's glidermen would come ashore on Utah Beach.

Even as their paratroop comrades were already fighting, at 0119 on 6 June, a flight of 52 planes belonging to the 434th Troop Carrier Wing took off from Aldermaston airbase. All towed Waco gliders. Flying the lead tow plane was the group commander while strapped in behind him was General Pratt. Unfortunately, during the form-up period, a glider containing the powerful SCR-449 command radio that General Maxwell Taylor was hoping to use to establish a direct radio link with England broke loose. Over France one plane and its glider were shot down while seven other tow planes and twenty-two gliders received hits from ground fire. Amazingly, 49 out of 50 pilots ignored the ground fire and released their gliders accurately at an altitude of 450 feet.

The first glider set down perfectly. Although the

Above: **Waco gliders, with their distinctive D-Day stripes, safely on the ground in Normandy.**

gliders could come to rest within 200 feet, the slick grass gave insufficient friction and the glider skidded across the field and crashed into a hedgerow. The impact killed the co-pilot and General Pratt (the highest ranking American to be killed on D-Day) while miraculously leaving the pilot conscious and alive. To the pilot's horror he saw that his glider's nose poked onto a lane where three German tanks were passing. Fortunately, the tanks ignored the wrecked glider. Subsequent gliders experienced shaky landings due to Rommel's "asparagus". Only six managed to set down at the designated landing zone (LZ), 15 set down within a half mile, 10 landed in a cluster far to the west, and 17 of the 18 remaining scattered to the east and southeast within two miles of the LZ E.

At 1830 that evening, 32 planes of the 434th Troop Carrier Group took off to begin Keokuk. Each towed a Horsa. Unknown to the pilots and glidermen, German infantry manned positions two miles north and two miles south of the designated landing zone. They opened fire as soon as the gliders separated from the tows. Some gliders landed amid German machine gun and mortar fire. Most of the gliders released at least a mile short of the LZ. German fire and accidents killed 14 men and caused 30 serious injuries.

Such was the 327th harrowing introduction to France in 1944.

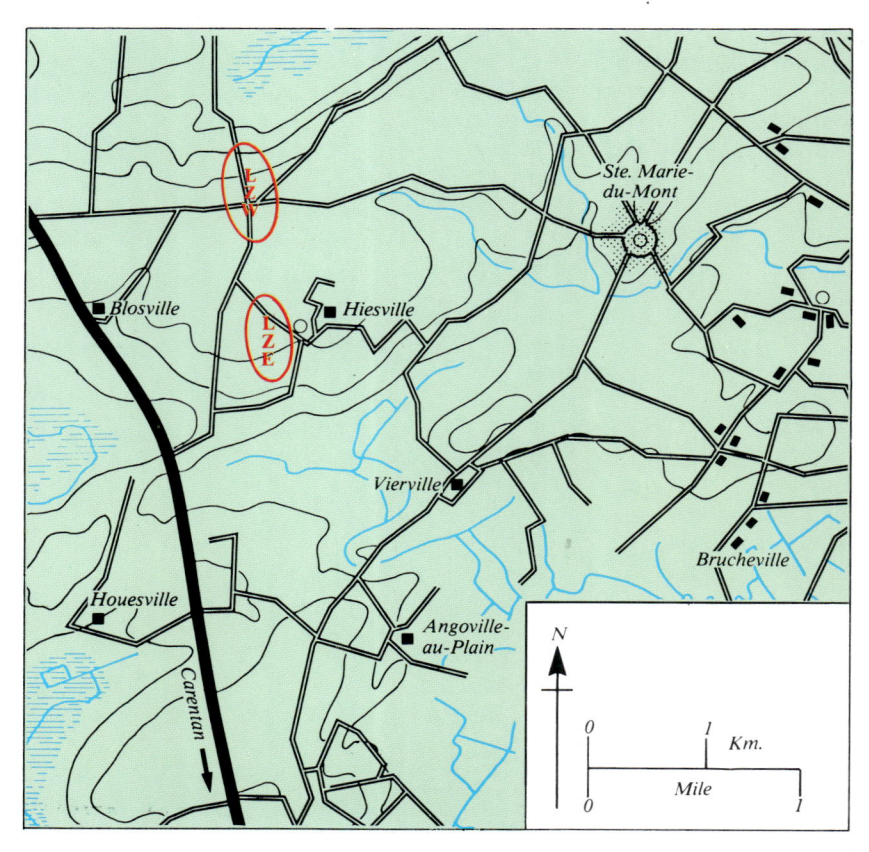

30

Allied Air Support

The parachute drop behind Utah Beach was the riskiest feature of the American cross-channel attack. The lives of some 13,000 paratroopers and glidermen were at stake. British General Leigh-Mallory was certain it would produce a disaster. General Omar Bradley conceded that the low-flying C-47s that would carry the paratroopers would encounter ground fire as soon as they made landfall over France, and that the gliders would have trouble in the Normandy hedgerows, but that the risks "must be subordinated to the importance of Utah Beach and the prompt capture of Cherbourg."

Complicating matters was the failure of Ninth Air Force ground personnel to assemble the necessary Waco gliders. Inexperienced and ill-equipped, they managed to assemble only one-third the quota by the end of 1943. When a wind storm destroyed 100 completed Wacos in March 1944, airborne planners realized that they might not have enough gliders to support the planned operations. By laboring seven days a week, with three shifts per day, workers managed to complete 910 Wacos by mid-April. However, only 288 of these had been fitted with the Griswold Nose crash protection devices. So hasty were preparations that the crews scheduled to fly the gliders and the transport aircraft did not assemble in England until the first week in March. The combination of glider shortage and late pilot assemblage meant that training had to be conducted in a great hurry. American pilots had a mere seven weeks to learn to fly the British-built Horsa gliders needed to land heavy equipment.

Planners required that the transport pilots attain a proficiency level that would allow them to deliver paratroops by night to within a mile of the drop zone and to fly glider missions by twilight or moonlight to a designated landing zone within one minute of schedule. During April, the 53d Troop Carrier Wing managed to cram in 6,965 hours of towing time in preparation for the glider landings. An exercise on 21 April proved that the tow pilots had well learned their craft when 241 out of 245 pilots released the gliders properly at the designated time.

A total of 822 transport planes flew from nine airfields to carry the men of the 82d and 101st Airborne Divisions into battle. The 53rd Troop Carrier Wing transported the 101st Airborne while the 50th Troop Carrier Wing conveyed the 82d Airborne. They took off before midnight and flew routes calculated to bring the first plane-loads in from the Cotentin peninsula's west side between 0115 and 0130. Preceding the main group by about 30 minutes were twenty pathfinder planes that were to land paratroopers to mark six drop zones and one landing zone. At dawn (H minus 2 hours) 51 gliders were to bring in special equipment while another 32 gliders were to land at dusk (H plus 15 hours). In the event, scattered cloud cover, enemy flak, and the inability of the pathfinders to mark all drop zones caused the parachute drops to become quite scattered.

Before H-Hour, scattered cloud cover also limited direct bombardment air missions on Utah Beach. Of the 360 medium bombers assigned to bomb seven objectives on Utah Beach, between 270 and 293 attacked while the remainder turned back without bombing because of their inability to see the target. They dropped nearly one-third of their 250-pound bombs seaward of the high water mark, thus missing any target. The bombing did little to neutralize or eliminate German coastal defense.

Because of overcast conditions and uncertainties about where stood the allied frontline, an anxiety heightened by the tremendous dispersal of airborne troops, tactical air support on D-Day was not dominant. During the days ahead this would change. The testament to the effectiveness of the allied air forces is the fact that on the American beaches, only two enemy fighters appeared to strafe the beaches during all of 6 June. The balance of the Luftwaffe had either been destroyed in previous fighting, forced to flee well inland to escape, or had been unable to penetrate the aerial curtain that allied fighters formed around the invasion beaches.

Far from the invasion beaches themselves, the allied air forces exerted decisive influence. For example, by 1600 on D-Day, when two reserve panzer divisions began to move toward Normandy, fighters and light bombers smashed everything that moved and forced the divisions to delay until nightfall. A mobile Kampfgruppen ordered out of nearby Brittany would take ten days to reach Normandy, so dominant were the allied air forces.

During 6 June, the Ninth Air Force fighters and bombers flew close to 3,000 sorties in tactical support of the 1st Army.

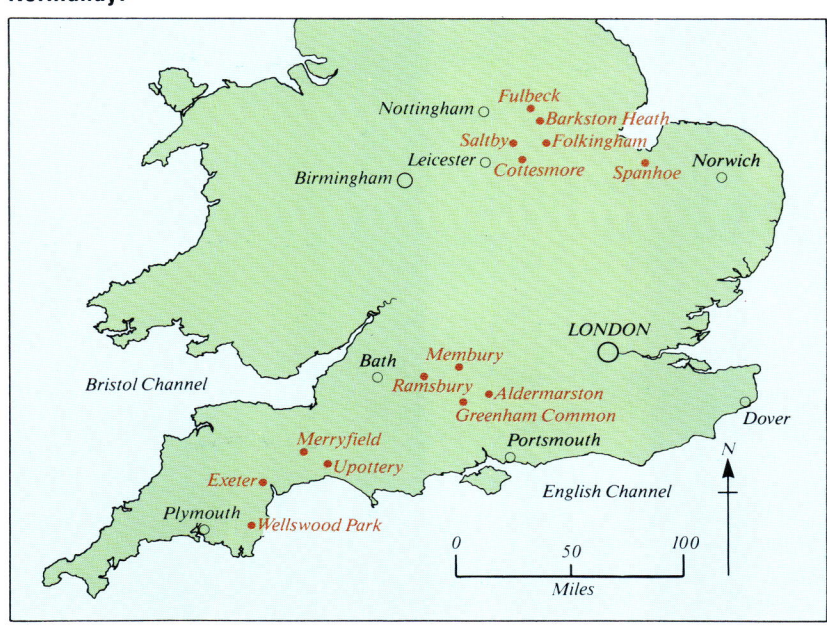

Above: **US Airborne troops prepare to board their Dakotas before the flight to France.**

Below: **The airfields used by the 9th Troop Carrier Command of the USAAF to fly the 82d and 101st Airborne Divisions to Normandy.**

Allied Naval Support

Task Force U, commanded by Rear Admiral Don P. Moon, USN, was part of the Western Naval Task Force led by Rear Admiral Alan G. Kirk. It comprised about 865 vessels and craft distributed in twelve convoys. Important to the ultimate success of Task Force U was the close cooperation between Admiral Moon and the commander of VII Corps, General Collins. Along with their staffs, these two officers jointly worked out the details for the navy's role in the attack on Utah Beach.

The naval effort to convoy the assault forces to the Normandy coast involved a complex minesweeping effort. Ten channels, each 400 to 1,200 yards wide, had to be swept through the German offshore minefields to permit the passage of the transport ships. Additional channels were cleared for the bombardment ships. The areas where the transports were to anchor also required sweeping. A total of 287 vessels performed mine sweeping duties of the allied invasion convoy. They were so successful that only one destroyer and one LST were mined during the channel crossing.

The second naval mission was to protect against any attacks by German light naval forces. German E-boats had successfully attacked one of the pre-invasion practices and caused heavy personnel losses. On D-Day, the boats of the 5th Flotilla out of Le Havre were intercepted by allied warships and driven back. A Norwegian destroyer was sunk during this encounter. Two torpedo boat flotillas based in Cherbourg sortied briefly and then returned to base because of heavy seas. This was the extent of German naval interference with allied D-Day operations.

The bombardment force had the formal mission "to assist in ensuring the safe and timely arrival of our forces by the engagement of hostile coastal defences". Toward this end the U.S. and British navies, supported by other allied forces, threw everything from battleships to rocket-firing support landing craft into the fray.

Bombardment Force A had one battleship, Pearl Harbor veteran *Nevada*, the monitor *Erebus*, five cruisers including two Dutch vessels, eight destroyers, and three subchasers organized into five fire support units. Force A's primary targets were the German batteries between Barfleur in the north to the mouth of the River Vire. The ships opened fire at 0550 and continued their bombardment for 40 minutes. Later, American naval officers would say this was not long enough. Still, these vessels delivered such accurate fire that they silenced the enemy coastal guns. The light cruiser *Enterprise*, the Dutch gunboat *Soemba* and eight destroyers remained close in shore to engage the German beach defenses. Later in the day, when one German battery resumed fire, it was quickly subdued by the overwhelming weight of fire delivered by the allied vessels.

The Task Force also featured a support group composing 33 light craft equipped with either rocket launchers or artillery. From positions close to shore these craft were to drench the beach with a final fire, the rockets being discharged when the infantry landing craft approached to within 700 yards of the beach.

The most serious problems came from the presence of a sandbank off the coast where the Germans had laid delayed-action mines. All of the D-Day losses including the USS *Corry*, a patrol vessel, and four landing craft came from these mines.

Once the troops cleared the beaches, they could count on receiving support for their inland attacks from the ships off the coast. Naval bombardment helped infantry and armor columns overcome German defenses both during D-Day and thereafter.

Some sense of the power of the allied bombardment can be gleaned from the D-Day report submitted to Rommel by the German commander of the Seventh Army: "Weapons sited in field works had to be dug out before use, owing to the preliminary bombardment of the enemy naval artillery. Coast defense guns were in most cases put out of action by direct hits on casemates. Counter-attacks... suffered very heavy casualties in the neighbourhood of the coast through enemy naval artillery fire." In fact, this German commander is partially making excuses for his failure. Direct hits against coastal batteries were rare. Instead, the naval barrage neutralized the coast defense guns. Of greater importance, particularly during the prolonged struggle to enlarge the beachhead, was the ability of naval artillery to break up enemy counterattacks before they closed to decisive range.

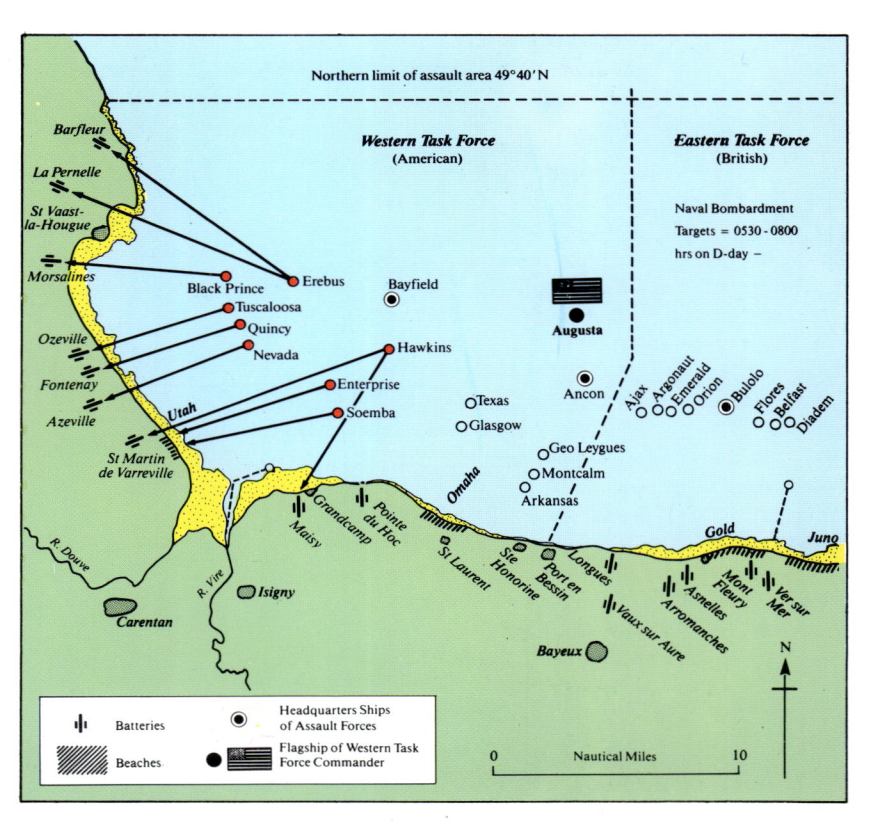

Below: **Allied warships tasked with the naval bombardment of the German targets on the Cotentin Peninsula in support of the landings on Utah beach.**